I0803625

Is Conformity to Customs Necessary in the Church?

Is Conformity to Customs Necessary in the Church?

An Exegetical Commentary on First Corinthians Eleven

By
Spiros Zodhiates, Th.D.

AMG
PUBLISHERS
Chattanooga, TN 37422

Is Conformity to Customs Necessary in the Church?

An Exegetical Commentary on First Corinthians Eleven

ISBN 0-89957-461-0

Printed in the United States of America
02 01 00 99 98 97 –R– 7 6 5 4 3 2 1

To Chuck Weaver,
a layman so dedicated to the learning of the Word of God that he taught himself the Greek language well enough to proofread many of my manuscripts.

Contents

Preface

In 1 Corinthians 9:1, 2, Paul asserts his apostolicity. In 1 Corinthians 11:2 he gives the Corinthian Christians certain instructions he wishes to be kept as he gives them. He does not want them to be changed to mere traditions. He does not want the Corinthians to pervert the commandments of God (*entolaí* [1785]) into human precepts (*entálmata* (1778]; cf. Matt. 15:1–9; Mark 7:1–23).

Paul deals with the mystery of the marriage of a man and a woman in the Lord (cf. 1 Cor. 7). He presents two individuals, a man and a woman, whom the Lord unites and forms into one body (Matt. 19:5; Mark 10:8). In the same way the Lord unites His bride (Rev. 18:23; 21:2, 9; 22:17), made of various saved people, to be united to Himself as the bridegroom (John 3:29) to form the church, His body (Eph. 5:32).

Paul expounds on the principle of headship (1 Cor. 11:3). As two people, a woman and a man become one in the Lord, having one head over two united bodies. If there are two heads, it is an indication that the union intended is not according to God's plan. Let it not be thought that when the two bodies become one body that the husband becomes the head and the wife remains as the body. They are still two individuals, but they are not equal (Gal. 3:28). Whereas they are two personalities, they are so united in purpose that it is as if they were one. Their state is similar to the person of the Godhead, who are separate persons but one being (John 10:30; 1 Cor. 11:3).

The oneness of essence is shown by the united direction given by God the Father wherein the husband, as ordained of God, becomes the head (1 Cor. 11:3). This is symbolically done by covering the wife's head, either by an artificial covering or by the natural covering of her hair. The husband needs no covering since his protection is Christ. The wife has double protection, that of her husband and that of Christ who protects them both. This is shown especially when a wife prays (1 Cor. 11:4–16).

The order ordained by God should be evident in public worship, where it should be obvious who of the worshipers belong to the male or female gender (1 Cor. 11:17–22).

The church's most significant gathering is the celebration of the Lord's Supper, for it speaks of His sacrifice and of its acceptance by the believers who participate. Through their worthy participation they show their declaration of unity with Him. They do not thereby become His members, but they show that they are His worthy members through faith. Holy communion is thus to be celebrated as a reminder of Christ's sacrifice for sinners until the time when the purpose of His sacrifice will have been accomplished when the season of grace reaches its end (1 Cor. 11:23–26).

The spirit of sacrifice ought to be demonstrated through the practice of sacrifice on the part of the believer. If we love others because they deserve it, we cannot claim we love the Lord Jesus as He loved us, for his love is a love of sacrifice. *Agápē* love is motivated by the need of others to experience what God has available for them, not because they deserve it, but because they need it. When we love others only because they deserve it, we participate of His sacrifice unworthily.

Unworthy participation in the Lord's supper may even result in physical death. But before we fall into such severe punishment, the Apostle Paul wants us to examine ourselves and be conscious of our participation in the feast of the sacrifice of Jesus Christ and by being imbued with the spirit of sacrifice (1 Cor. 11:27–34).

May the Apostle Paul's purpose of writing 1 Corinthians 11 be accomplished in all who read this book.

SPIROS ZODHIATES

An Overview of First Corinthians

Author:	Paul the Apostle, author of thirteen other epistles to various individuals and congregations.
Date:	About A.D. 55.
Recipients:	The congregation Paul had established in Corinth.
Place:	From Ephesus
Theme:	Paul had received news about the Corinthian brethren from several sources (1 Cor. 1:11; 7:1; 16:17). The church was afflicted with many of the problems that face young churches and new converts. The Apostle, under the inspiration of the Holy Spirit, decided to write this urgent letter to admonish and instruct the church. Among other topics he discussed: the necessity of church discipline (5:1–13); divisions and disputes among Christians (1:10–16; 6:1–11); matters of conscience (8:1–13; 10:19–33); the support of preachers (9:1–27); abuses of the Lord's Supper (10:16–17, 21; 11:17–34); the misuse of spiritual gifts (12:1—14:40); and the importance of the resurrection of Jesus Christ (15:1–58).

An Outline of First Corinthians

In the days of the Apostle Paul, Corinth was the capital city of the Roman province of Achaia and the glory of Greece. Though its great ancient splendor had been destroyed by the Romans in 120 B.C., the city was rebuilt under Julius Caesar and restored to wealth and luxury under Augustus. Among all the cities of the world, however, it was most well known for its lewdness. The Apostle Paul lived in Corinth for eighteen months (Acts 18:11). After his departure, Paul went to Ephesus. During his three-year stay there, he heard reports of wickedness and division within the Corinthian church. In an effort to correct these evils, Paul wrote several letters to them, including the Epistle of First Corinthians.

1:1–9	The introductory remarks of Paul.
1:10–16	Paul condemns the divisions in the church and exhorts its members to unity.
1:17—2:16	Paul defends his ministry. He has preached the wisdom of Christ crucified. This wisdom is foolishness to the world, but is the glory of all those to whom the Spirit of God has revealed the truthfulness of it.
3:1–5	Paul declares that the simplicity of his teaching was due to the carnal state of the Corinthians, which state is clearly evidenced by their divisions.
3:6–23	Jesus Christ is the only foundation. Ministers are mere servants; the work is God's.
4:1–6	The duty of ministers is faithfulness.
4:6–21	Paul contrasts the arrogance and conceit of the false teachers to the humility and sacrifice of the apostles. Using his unique position as their spiritual father, Paul calls on the Corinthian believers to be discerning.
5:1–13	Flagrant, sexual immorality was being practiced by one of the members of the congregation. Paul reproves

	their lack of discipline and calls for expulsion of the guilty party.
6:1–11	Christians should not bring their legal disputes before heathen judges.
6:12–20	Paul reprimands the perversion of the principle of Christian liberty to excuse fornication. Our bodies belong to the Lord and should be devoted to His glory.
7:1–17	Paul answers their questions about marriage.
7:18–24	Paul advises that, provided they are not immoral or unlawful, our social positions should remain intact after coming to Christ.
7:25–40	Paul answers their questions about virgins and widows.
8:1–13	Christian liberty and conscience: was it lawful to eat meat that had been sacrificed to false gods?
9:1–23	Paul declares the right of ministers to be faithfully supported by their congregation.
9:24—10:13	Exhortations to self-denial.
10:14—11:1	While the purchase of meat offered to idols is a matter of conscience, attendance at the heathen feasts of sacrifice is idolatry, even if such was not their intention.
11:2–16	Men and women should take care to conform to the customs of dress in their community that assure modesty and properly reflect the man to be "the glory of God" and the woman to be "the glory of the man."
11:17–34	Paul exhorts the Corinthians to properly partake of the Lord's Supper.
12:1–31	Paul answers their questions about spiritual gifts. He reminds them that they are all members of one body. God has distributed these gifts so that each member may perform the function it is designed for.

13:1–13	Love [*agápe* {26}] is superior to all other gifts.
14:1–25	The gift of prophecy is more valuable than the gift of tongues.
14:26–40	Principles for orderly public worship.
15:1–34	Paul proves the fact of the resurrection of Christ. It is the foundation of our faith and the surety of our own resurrection.
15:35–58	Paul explains the nature of our resurrection.
16:1–9	Paul's specific instructions for the collection of monies from several Greek congregations for the poverty-stricken saints in Palestine.
16:10–12	Recommendations for Timothy and Apollos to be accepted by the Corinthians.
16:13–24	Paul's final admonition to them to stand firm in the faith. Salutation.

1 Cor. 11:1 | Imitate Me Even as I Imitate Christ

"Keep becoming imitators of me, even as I am of Christ."

In 1 Corinthians 4:1–5, Paul makes a plea for believers to live consecrated, self-sacrificing lives, in spite of the likelihood of being criticized. Then in verses 6 to 21 he compares the easy lives of the Corinthians with the self-denying lifestyle of the Apostles. And in verse 16, he states, "I beseech you, therefore, become imitators of me."

Going on in chapter 5, Paul details a situation of immorality in the church, and how the church should deal with it. He advises them not to cover up the sin of the immoral person, but to seek a redemptive method to restore him.

In chapter 6, he acknowledges that in the Christian church there will be differences that will tempt believers to go to court against other believers. He pinpoints the problem, however, when he tells them that the root of this evil is greed for material things (*biōtiká* [982]; see vv. 3, 4). Then in verse 10 he asserts that greedy people, among other sinners, will not inherit the kingdom of God.

In chapter 7, Paul handles marriage as a sacred right of every believer, but he explains why he personally preferred to stay single. His reason for a celibate life was to have more time and freedom to work for the Lord, as his passion of life was to win as many as possible to Jesus Christ (7:32–35).

In chapters 8 through 10, Paul handles some matters of life which, although mundane, prove to be divisive among Christians. When some unbelievers observe such divisions among true believers, they may reject the most important and basic experience of regeneration. In these three chapters, Paul has given himself as an example. The major things in his life were to win souls to Christ (9:19–23), to maintain the unity of the Spirit among believers (Eph. 4:3, 13), and to avoid fighting for one's own rights. The rights of every believer, including the apostles, are to be subjugated to this passion of winning souls to Christ and the means to make this possible (9:1–5, 19). Paul's philosophy of life can be summarized in one simple phrase: Do not live selfishly.

"Keep Becoming Imitators of Me"

The unimportant things in the Christian life are known as the *adiáphora*, nonessentials. In concluding how to handle these nonessentials, Paul urges the Corinthians to imitate him as he imitated Christ. While in 1 Corinthians 4:16, he wrote, "I beseech you, therefore, become imitators of me," in this verse, which should be the conclusion of this whole discussion concerning the unimportant things of Christian behavior, he adds a very important detail: "**even as I *am* of Christ.**" Had Paul's life not been one of self-denial and sacrifice in imitation of Christ, he would not have had the right to say, "Become imitators of me."

The verb which is used by Paul is not "be" imitators of me, but "become" (*gínesthe*, the second person plural present middle deponent imperative of *gínomai* [1096], to become [1 Cor. 4:16; Eph. 5:1, cf. 1 Thess. 1:6, 2:14]). The verb *gínomai* indicates that the Christian life is a progressive moral and spiritual journey toward maturity once a believer has the nature of God indwelling him (2 Pet. 1:4). Before one can begin to grow spiritually, he must acquire life by becoming a child of God (John 1:12; 1 John 3:9). This is mandated, for who is not deeply grieved if his child does not grow and mature? One way we mature is by observing the behavior of those who have made progress in the maturation process. Although maturity never reaches a point of perfection in the Christian life, one should imitate Christians who have grown in the Lord more than themselves and learn from them. There is a reason the Apostle Paul does not use the aorist imperative *genethḗte*, become. He instead uses the present imperative *gínesthe*, be becoming, which indicates continuity. There is no arrival point to a believer's maturity. It is progressive, always "becoming." A Christian can never stop becoming what Christ was. He must be aware of the fact that no man can become what Christ was, for He alone was God (John 1:1).

Unfortunately, some translators have rendered *mimētaí*, the nominative plural masculine of *mimētḗs* (3402), imitator, as "followers." A *mimētḗs* can be a follower only if he has the nature of God and is born from above (John 3:3, 7). The verb "to imitate" is *miméomai* (3401) which has an entirely different meaning than the verb "to follow" (*akolouthéō* [190]). We read in Scripture that the multitudes followed Him (Matt. 4:25; 8:1). One can follow Christ in the sense of coming after Him, but he must be a child of God in order to imitate Christ. Paul could not be an imitator of Christ had it not been for the Damascus experience (Acts 9:3–19; 22:6–16; 26:12–18).

"Even as I *Am* of Christ"

Observe that Paul says, "Even as I of Christ." There is no verb in this phrase, but the verb that was used previously in the present imperative must also be implied here. It would be wrong to say that the implied tense of the verb is the perfect tense, "as I have become of Christ," for that would imply that Paul speaks of his arrival at maturity in Christ, and not of his progressive march toward it.

In 1 Corinthians 11:1, Paul says, "Even as I am becoming of Christ." This is an indirect way of saying that Christ, whom he seeks to imitate in every instance of his life, is God. It is an affirmation of the deity of Jesus Christ. The life of Jesus Christ was not merely the life of a good man here on earth, but the life of the incarnate God. Since we are God's beloved children (Eph. 5:1) and have His nature within us (2 Pet. 1:4; 1 John 3:9), He gives us the power to grow in Him and become like Him. The full verse of Ephesians 5:1 says, "Therefore, continue to become imitators of God [the Father], as beloved children [*tékna* {5043} from the verb *tíktō* {5088}, to give birth to]." It is interesting to note that Jesus Christ is never called "the child of God," but "the Son" (*huiós* [5207], son, one who has conscious agreement with his father). When man becomes an imitator of the incarnate Christ, he becomes an imitator of God the Father.

In Ephesians 5:1, Paul said, "Therefore, keep becoming [*gínesthe*] imitators of *the* God." Note that the definite article "the" precedes the word *Theoú* (God) which refers to God the Father.

In 1 Thessalonians 1:6, Paul writes, "You also became [*egenḗthēte*, the second person plural aorist passive deponent indicative of *gínomai*, to become] our imitators and of the Lord." Then he goes on to give a characteristic instance of why he also adds, "of the Lord, having received the Word **in much affliction** with joy of the Holy Spirit." One way in which we can become imitators of the Lord Jesus Christ and Paul is to receive the Word even if it causes us to suffer affliction. We are able to do this by the power of the Holy Spirit. Both Jesus Christ and the Apostle Paul as His servant suffered for the sake of the gospel. What do we do as Christian believers when we are engulfed in tribulation and suffering? How we behave in tribulation shows the depth of our spiritual maturity.

The same note is struck in 1 Thessalonians 2:14: "For you, brethren, became [*egenḗthēte*] imitators [*mimētaí*] of the churches of God which in Judea are in Christ Jesus: **for you also have suffered like things** of your own countrymen, even as I have of the Jews." To suffer at the hands of your own countrymen without complaint is to imitate both Christ and His church.

LESSONS:

1. There is a difference between being a follower of Christ and an imitator of Him.
2. An imitator of Christ must first have the nature of God within him; in other words, he must be born again.
3. The believer never ceases to grow spiritually and to mature in Christ.
4. Jesus Christ was God incarnate, and although the child of God acquires the nature of God, he does not become a god. That there are things that we cannot do which Christ did is due to the fact that we are not Christ. Instead of praying that we would be able to do as Christ did, we should ask the Lord what He would have us, as His children, do.

1 Cor. 11:2 | Paul Commends and Recommends

But I commend you, brethren, that in all things you remember me, and keep faithfully the traditions as I delivered them to you.

Paul had given some fundamental principles in the previous chapters of 1 Corinthians to guide the believers in the conduct of their lives, and especially two pieces of advice which are basic tenants of the walk of faith. The first one is found in 1 Corinthians 10:24: "Let no one keep seeking his own good, but each one *seek* that which is another's, *although it is* different." The second is found in verse 32: "Continue to be without offense."

"But I Commend You, Brethren"

The fact that the Corinthian believers received Paul's recommendations was worthy of commendation. Paul had given them guidelines regarding conduct in society and in the church, and now he commends them for receiving his fatherly advice.

The word for "commend" is *epainṓ*, the first person singular present active indicative of *epainéō* (1867), to praise, commend, and it is derived from the preposition *epí* (1909), upon, and *ainéō* (134), to praise. This verb is found also in verse 17: "Now in this that I declare unto you I praise [*epainṓ*] you not, and that you come together not for the better, but for the worse." What is translated "in this I declare unto you" is the verb *paraggéllōn*, the nominative singular masculine present active participle of *paraggéllō* (3853), I beseech, I recommend. The word "not" is the absolute negative *ouk* (3756). Clearly, Paul does not want the Corinthians to misunderstand his recommendations as commendations! In verse 22, he says, "What! Have you not houses to eat and to drink in? Or do you despise the church of God, and shame them that have not? What shall I say to you? Shall I praise [*epainésō*, the first person singular aorist active subjunctive mood of *epainéō*] you in this? I praise [*epainṓ*] you not." Paul could not commend the turning of the celebration of the Lord's Supper into a mere opportunity to eat, and he chides the Corinthians for allowing this to happen rather than remembering the Lord's suffering and death for them. Furthermore, Paul rebukes the Corinthians for embarassing those who did not have enough food to eat.

"That in All Things You Remember Me"

Although Paul had many recommendations for the Corinthian Christians, he had only a few things for which he could commend them. The fact that they always remembered him was worthy of commendation. Who could forget the Apostle Paul and his sacrificial ministry in Corinth?

The verb used in this phrase is *mémnēsthe*, the second person plural perfect passive indicative of *mimnḗskō* (3043), to recall to one's mind. A more accurate translation would be, "You have been bringing me to your minds." It is as if the Apostle Paul were saying that no matter what problem they faced, they recalled his teaching concerning that particular problem. Thus he urges, "Keep becoming imitators of me as I am of Christ." The Corinthians kept alive Paul's counsel and recommendations. They had not forgotten, because they recognized that he had given them godly counsel.

"And Keep Faithfully the Traditions"

The second part of the verse advises the Corinthians that their memory should be activated in a faithful manner: "And as I delivered to you the traditions, hold them fast [or faithfully]." We must bear in mind that the punctuation marks were not in the original text, and the comma that is placed in the Greek after *humín*, to you (the dative plural second person of the personal pronoun *sú* [4771], you), should be after the word *paradóseis* (3862), traditions. The verb *katéchete* (2722), to hold fast or hold down faithfully, should be taken as an imperative and not as a present indicative. Morphologically it could be either an indicative or an imperative. If it were taken as an imperative, it would read as follows: "And as I delivered to you the traditions, hold [them] faithfully." It is impossible for Paul to say in 1 Corinthians 11:17, 22 that he absolutely did not commend the Corinthians; however, in 11:2 his commendation was very restricted. The fact that they did not forget his teaching, but brought it to the forefront every time they faced a problem in society or in the church, was evident. That they held faithfully those doctrines or those traditions which Paul gave to them without changing them was a conditional commendation. Evidently Paul still had reservations regarding the Corinthian Christians.

The word "traditions" needs careful examination since there has been considerable misunderstanding as to its actual meaning. It is translated from *paradóseis*, the plural of *parádosis*, delivery, and is that which is delivered directly from its source or passed along as accurately as it was originally transmitted. The noun derives from *paradídōmi* (3860), to deliver. *Parádosis* originally referred to the act of transmitting an event or teaching, and not that which was transmitted. However, over the years, it also has come to mean that which is transmitted. Paul was concerned that, as in doctrines of the past, many additions or alterations had been made, and he wanted the Corinthians to understand the desire of the transmitter and guard against such alterations. They were to make sure that they used the original transmission as their guide.

In the New Testament we find two Greek words that are derived from the same verb, *entéllomai* (1781), to command, which is from the preposition *en* (1722), in, upon, and *teléō* (5055), to accomplish, charge, command, akin to *télos* (5056), goal, and *téllō*, to set out for a definite point or goal. The compound verb means to order, to command, or enjoin upon. The noun derived from the verb is *éntalma* (1778), rule, precept. It is unfortunate, however, that in Matthew 15:9 and Mark 7:7 in the King James Version the word is translated "commandments." The New International Version, however, translates it as "traditions." The only other passage in which this word occurs is Colossians 2:22 where again the King James Version translates *entálmata* as "commandments," the New International Version as "rules taught by men." *Entálmata* referred to human rules invented by the Pharisees and scribes who transmitted the law of God with many expansions and embellishments. Christ, therefore, spoke of these precepts as human rules (*entálmata*), or the "tradition of the elders" (Matt. 15:2; Mark 7:3). The Lord Jesus said to the Pharisees in Matthew 15:3, "Why do you also transgress the commandment [*entolḗn*, the accusative of *entolḗ* {1785}, commandment] of God by your tradition [*parádosin*]?" It is evident that tradition came to mean something that was not in agreement with the commandment of God. In Matthew 15:6, the Lord Jesus accuses the Pharisees and scribes of having annulled the commandment of God by their tradition: "Thus have you made the commandment [*entolḗn*] of God of none effect [*ēkurṓsate*, the second person plural aorist active indicative of *akuróō* {208}, to cancel, annul] by your tradition [*parádosin*]" (cf. Mark 7:3, 5, 8). In Mark 7:9, the Lord accuses them of rejecting the commandment of God so that they may keep their traditions.

"Tradition," then, came to mean not the law of God itself, but man-made rules and regulations. As A. C. Zenos says in *A Dictionary of Christ and the Gospels*, edited by J. Hastings,

> The teachings of men came to take the place which belonged to those of God. It could not go further back than the elders (fathers), and those who were called upon to accept it must do so upon the authority of human statements. Tradition, thus, canonized the media communication, and lost sight of the value and validity of the things communicated on one side, and of the authority of Him from whom the communication came on the other. Whatever the claim for the Divine origin of the Mishna [a reiteration of the Mosaic Law] might be, the practical result of its acceptance was the exaltation of the means through which it came to the supreme place of authority. [Vol. 2, p. 741 under the article "Tradition"]

"As I Delivered *Them* to You"

Another word that should be examined closely because it has brought confusion and division in the Christian church is the verb *parédōka*, the first person singular aorist active indicative of *paradídōmi*, to deliver over to someone. This comes from the preposition *pará* (3844), from (implying that the teachings or traditions were delivered from the Apostle Paul directly to the Corinthians), and *dídōmi* (1325), to give. Paul never gave so much advice regarding a Christian's behavior in society and in the church as he did to the Corinthians! He stated in 1 Corinthians 15:3, "For I delivered [*parédōka*] unto you first of all that which I also received [*parélabon*, the first person singular second aorist active indicative of *paralambánō* {3880}], how that Christ died for our sins according to the Scriptures." The preposition *pará*, which is the prefix of the verbs *paradídōmi* and *paralambáno*, denotes the closest possible proximity. Paul is saying that he received the traditions or doctrines directly from the Lord and gave them directly to the Corinthians. Although Paul had delivered the gospel to the Corinthians as he had directly received it from the Lord, the Corinthians rendered it as mere rules and regulations that did not bear likeness to the words of the Lord that Paul had delivered to them. Hence his advice in 1 Corinthians 11:2 is to hold faithfully (*katéchō*, hold fast) the doctrines or traditions as he had delivered them originally, and not as they had evolved. In 2 Thessalonians 2:15 Paul also urged the Thessalonians to do likewise:

> Therefore, brethren, stand fast, and hold [*krateíte*, the second person plural present active imperative of *kratéō* {2902}, to hold fast, preserve which implies unaltered] the traditions [*paradóseis*] which you were taught [*edidáchthēte*, the second person plural aorist passive indicative of *didáskō* {1321}, to teach which implies as you were taught] whether by word, or our epistle.

Paul's plea to them was to carefully preserve the oral teachings even though they were not yet put in writing. He also deals with this subject in 2 Thessalonians 3:6:

> Now we command you, brethren, in the name of our Lord Jesus Christ, that you withdraw yourselves from every brother that walks disorderly, and not after the tradition [*parádosin*] which he received [*parélabe*, TR, the third person singular aorist active indicative of *paralambánō*, to receive directly; cf. 1 Cor. 15:3 where we find the verbs *parédōka*, personally delivered, and *parélabon*, I received directly] of us.

The truth that is implied here is that a person who does not adhere to the tradition or the teaching as delivered by Paul has gone astray.

Paul describes his preconversion experience as one in which he was "more exceedingly zealous of the traditions of my fathers" (Gal. 1:14). In other words, he was a fanatic in defending that which he received from his fathers concerning the Jewish religion, yet he was far from understanding the grace of God and far from knowing and showing the love of Christ.

LESSONS:

1. The word *epaínō* (1867), I commend, is used only once by Paul, and that is in 1 Corinthians 11:2. But was there really anything for which he could commend the Corinthians fervently? In 1 Corinthians 11:17, 22, he said that he absolutely did not commend them. The only thing that he could find for which he could commend them in our verse is the fact that his teaching among them was not forgotten.
2. Paul carefully instructed the Corinthians regarding their lives in the heathen society in which they lived and in the Corinthian church.
3. He was concerned that they keep the traditions, unaltered, as he had given them.
4. The verb *katéchete* (2722) is the present imperative, not the present indicative of the verb *katéchō*, to hold fast or faithfully, and is thus a command for daily living.
5. The teaching of Paul could not contradict the teaching of Christ who castigated the Pharisees and scribes for trying to enforce their own human traditions over and against the laws of God (Matt. 15:1–9; Mark 7:1–13).

1 Cor. 11:3 | *The Concept of Headship*

> *But I want you to realize that the head of every husband is Christ, and the head of the wife is the husband, and the head of Christ is God.*

As Paul begins his discussion of head coverings, what does he want to convey to the Corinthians? Precepts such as the ones we will now study can be understood only by believers who are indwelt by the Spirit of God and are able to think with their spiritually illumined intelligence. It is extremely difficult for people who are not spiritually minded to understand and submit to the principles that Paul expounds in the following verses.

"But I Want You to Realize"

The verb with which this verse begins is *thélō* (2309), I will, I wish, I desire, and it implies active volition and purpose. This is the only time in this entire chapter that Paul expresses a personal desire. In the Greek text, the verb is followed by the adversative *dé* (1161), but. What we have translated as "to realize," or to perceive, is *eidénai*, the perfect active infinitive of *eídō* (1492) which is used in the present tense meaning to know intuitively. Hence, our translation "I want you [*humás*, the accusative plural second person of the personal pronoun *sú* {4771}] to realize [or to perceive]." Paul, in other words, declares that this concept can only be comprehended spiritually. Furthermore, among God's creation, only man is uniquely endowed with the ability to perceive such precepts and draw conclusions.

"That the Head"

What is this principle that Paul wants the Corinthians to understand? It is the principle of headship.

In Greek, as in English, some words have two meanings. The word *anḗr* (435) can mean either a man or a husband, and the word *gunḗ* (1135) can mean either a woman or a wife. We must use the context to determine the meanings these words convey. Each time that we encounter these two words, it is necessary to find out if they have the more expanded meaning of man or woman, or the more restrictive meaning of husband or wife. In deciding upon the meaning of these words, we acknowledge that we have no definitive way to know which meaning is correct other than judging from the general context in which the words are found.

There is another word, *ánthrōpos* (444), man, which generically means a human being without distinction as to whether it is male or female. The noun, however, is masculine. When it comes to the word *gunḗ*, it is the only word used for both a female human being and a wife.

In the context of 1 Corinthians 11, a very definite distinction is made between the words *anḗr* and *gunḗ* as a man and a woman. The noun *anḗr* occurs fourteen times, and the word *gunḗ* occurs sixteen times. The main reason for using these two words is to draw attention to the distinction between men and women as God created them and assigned to each a unique purpose to fulfill in life. Any unbiased reader of this chapter must conclude that the Apostle encourages us, as redeemed human beings, to respect the distinctness and uniqueness of the genders which

God made. Furthermore, this chapter teaches us that we, as human beings, have no right to hide our identity or to try to change it because it has been predetermined by God.

God designed a male and a female so that He could form them into one in the bond of marriage. Jesus taught, "They shall be the two into one flesh" (Matt. 19:5; Mark 10:9). The Apostle Paul confirmed that it was, indeed, God's desire to unify a male and a female to bring about a unique union while still maintaining the individuality of each person (Eph. 5:31).

Once this miracle of marriage takes place, when a born-again man takes unto him a born-again woman and they become one unit, they become endowed with a quality of oneness given by God. Paul, in Galatians 3:28, says, "there is neither male nor female, for you are all one in Christ Jesus." Two observations ought to be made on this particular verse. First, the word for "male" here is *ársen*, the accusative singular neuter adjectival form of *ársēn* or *árrēn* (730), and the word for "female" is *thēlu*, the accusative singular neuter adjectival form of *thḗlus* (2338), female. These two words refer to the original creation of man into male and female and speak of God's sovereignty in creation. Genesis 2:21-24 tells us how the first female was created:

> And the Lord God caused a deep sleep to fall upon Adam, and he slept; and He took one of his ribs, and closed up the flesh instead thereof. And the rib, which the Lord God had taken from man, made He a woman, and brought her unto the man. And Adam said, "This is now bone of my bones, and flesh of my flesh: she shall be called Woman, because she was taken out of Man." Therefore shall a man leave his father and his mother, and shall cleave unto his wife: and they shall be one flesh.

In Galatians 3:28, at the same time that Paul says, "There is neither male nor female," he also says, "There is neither Jew nor Greek, there is neither bond nor free." At that time, there was a distinction made between those who came from the Jewish race and those from Gentile nations. There were also those who were free and those who were slaves. Through Christ's redemptive work, He was able to take these diverse groups of people and cause them to become one in Himself. This is why, at the end of this verse, we read, "For you are all one in Christ Jesus." The word "one" is *heís* (1520), one, a unity, which is miraculously formed by Christ who is God.

God created the male before He created the female. There had to be a first in all things. But if we think of the first as being only privilege, the Apostle Peter in 1 Peter 3:7 gives us the reason that God, in His infinite wisdom and sovereignty, created the male before the female:

> Likewise you husbands [*ándres,* the plural of *anḗr,* here correctly translated "husbands"] dwell with them [the wives] according to knowledge, giving honor [*timḗn,* the accusative singular feminine noun of *timḗ* {5092}, attributed value, intimating that a woman selected to be a man's wife should be given special attributed value and honor] as unto the weaker vessel, and as being heirs together of the grace of life; that your prayers be not hindered.

Thus, the wife's depends on her husband because she is weaker and he is stronger, and they were designed so by God. The word "strong" should not be interpreted as superior, but as physically stronger and thus protective and responsible; and "weak" not as inferior, but as physically weaker and in need of love and protection. In His infinite wisdom, God has not done anything out of caprice, but out of design and purpose. Thus we can say that God made the male strong and the female weak so that in the union of marriage the husband can provide for and protect the wife, and the wife can help and uphold her husband.

"Of Every Husband Is Christ"

Thus, when Paul says that Christ is the head of every man, he does not mean man as an individual, but as a husband in the mystical union of marriage. This is the reason we translated *andrós* "husband," instead of using the general term "man."

The adjective *pantós*, the genitive singular neuter adjectival form of *pás* (3956), everyone, must be qualified to mean everyone belonging to the group of the redeemed. Certainly, it cannot be taken as referring to the totality of humanity, but to the totality of redeemed humanity. And when referring to redeemed humanity, we must restrict it even further to the men who have become husbands. What is Christ to every husband? He is the head (*kephalḗ* [2776], head, the nominative singular feminine noun).

We should take note of another word in 1 Peter 3:7 which has been rendered as "heirs together." This is translated from *sugklēronómoi*, the nominative plural masculine adjectival form of *sugklēronómos*, (4789), fellow heir, derived from the preposition *sún* (4862), together, conjointly, and *klēronómos* (2818), heir. Peter wants us to realize that because wives are physically weaker does not mean that they are less heirs together of the grace of life than husbands. In fact, the wife is a double recipient of the grace of Christ for she enjoys not only the love and grace of her Lord, but also the love and care which her husband is to provide for her (Eph. 5:25, 28; Col. 3:19). Weakness can be advantageous! In a visit to the Yosemite National Park we stared in disbelief that trees of such magnitude and age existed. One of the Sequoia trees is estimated to be 2,700 years old. Its diameter is about 35 feet. How is it that these massive trees were spared the timberman's axe? Massive though they may be, they have a weakness that is their protection. When one of these giants falls to the ground, it shatters into many pieces, thus rendering it useless for timber. Its survival lies in its weakness.

There is a uniqueness to the headship of Christ in a marriage bond. In Ephesians 5:32, Paul calls marriage "a mystery" equal to the mystery of the church. If the marriage of two different people and their ability to live together and to live for one another is called a mystery, how much more mysterious is the church where many people are enabled by Christ to live together in harmony and peace?

We see Christ is called the head of the church in Ephesians 1:23. Then in Colossians 1:18, 24 the church is called the body of Jesus Christ. One reason many marriages are monstrosities is the lack of recognition of the headship of Christ and of the headship of the husband in marriage. They are one body with two heads. Our Lord and Paul indicate that there can be only one head per body, whether that body is formed from two or many. As the marriage and the church are called mysteries (Eph. 5:31, 32), Christ is also called a mystery, Someone that we cannot fully understand. In fact, Ephesians 3:4 speaks of the mystery of Christ.

There is the definite article "the" (*ho* [3588]) in front of the word "Christ," which gives uniqueness to Him. "**The** Christ" ought to be "**the** head" of every husband, and then the blessing intended by God on the marriage can be given.

"The Christ" means "the Messiah." It is the divine name of Jesus Christ. He is to be recognized and accepted as God, actively participating in the marriage of two individuals if the wife is to accept her husband as head of the union. The head is a representative part of the whole personality. Paul, in Acts 18:6, said to the persecuting Corinthians, "Your blood be upon your own heads."

Christ should have full control of a marriage through the husband as he is conscious that the Lord is the moving and intelligent force guiding him.

"And the Head of *the* Wife *Is* the Husband"

If we accept this phrase as translated in the King James Version and other translations designating the two words of gender as "woman" and "man," it is in direct contradiction to what Paul says in Galatians 3:28: "There is neither male nor female." It makes sense, however, to say that "the head of every wife is the husband."

In what way is the husband the head of the wife? In the New Testament there are two verbs that are used to indicate the propriety of interrelationships. There is the verb meaning to obey which is *hupakoúō* (5219) and derives from *hupó* (5259), under, beneath, and *akoúō* (191), to hear, hearken. It means to yield to a superior command or force without necessarily being willing. It is used of the wind and sea tempest (Matt. 8:27; Mark 4:41; Luke 8:15), and also of unclean spirits (Mark 1:27). In human relationships, it is used of children's obedience to parents. In Ephesians 6:1, we read, "Children obey [*hupakoúete*] your parents in the Lord: for this is right" (cf. Col. 3:20). The verb, however, is never used of a wife in relationship to her husband. Another word is used for that relationship, and it is *hupotássomai*, the middle voice of *hupotássō* (5293). The active verb means to put oneself in the category in which he or she belongs, and the middle voice *hupotássomai* means to place oneself under the category where one perceives that he or she belongs. The basic verb *tássō* (5021) means to arrange in order. The noun *táxis* (5010) is order, rank, arrangement. This verb *hupotássomai*, to take one's proper order or position under, is the verb that is used to indicate the attitude of wives toward their own husbands (Eph. 5:22; Col. 3:18; 1 Pet. 3:1, 5; Titus 2:5), for it involves the understanding and the submission of a wife to God's design and thus to God's order. God put the wife under the husband's love and care and protection, making the husband the head of the wife. This, however, does not mean that the wife is an inferior creation of God. They are both human beings with equal access to God their creator and Christ their redeemer. Each has a will to be exercised in his or her accomplishments of God's design for mankind and the mystery of marriage. What we have between the husband and wife is orderly equality. In marriage there is a triangle. The apex is Christ with the sides being the husband and wife, thus making Christ the head of both.

"The Head of Christ *Is* God [the Father]"

The word "God" (*Theós* [2316]) with a definite article (in this case *ho*, the) before it means the Father (John 1:1). Christ is the divine name of the eternal Son of God, meaning the Messiah who is coequal and coeternal with the Father. He has always been with the Father (John 1:18). But why is the Father called the head of Christ? Is it because Christ in His eternal existence is inferior to the Father? Jesus, describing His mediatorial work in John 10:29, said, "My Father, which gave them Me, is greater [*meízōn* {3187}, the nominative singular masculine comparative adjectival form of *mégas* {3173}, great] than all; and no man is able to pluck them out of My Father's hand." However, to show that the Father's greatness is not ontological but functional, the Lord adds, "I and My Father are one [*hén*, the accusative singular neuter numeral of *heís*, one]." He implies that They are of one essence, Deity, not one person since He differentiated between Himself and the Father in verse 29. Jesus affirmed that Christ and the Father are two different Persons, but they are one essence (John 7:16). The Father sent Christ, and Christ was faithful in executing the purpose for which He was sent. The relationship that exists between the two eternal Persons in no way renders the One inferior to the Other. To understand this eternal functional difference of the Father and the Son, one must study what the Apostle Paul states in 1 Corinthians 15:24–28.

Paul wants us to understand that the relationship between husband and wife in Christian marriage is similar to that of the Father and Son. As the head of Christ is the Father, the head of the wife is the husband, but that does not make the wife inferior. They are one flesh (Matt. 19:5; Mark 10:8; Eph. 5:31), but functionally different.

This simile is evident through God's redemptive creation. There is Christ and there is the Father, and the Father is stated to be the head of this eternal relationship. It does not mean that the Father is ontologically greater than Christ the Son, but functionally in the mediatorial work of the Son.

Paul presents this equality between the sexes as basic to his discussion. The difference is only functional and must be followed as God designed it, or the results of disobedience will be catastrophic. There cannot be two functional authorities where there is more than one personality involved. So what Paul says in 1 Corinthians 11:3 fully agrees with what he says in Galatians 3:28, "There is neither male or female." However, in Galatians, Paul speaks not necessarily of husband and wife, but of male and female because the body of Christ is made up of men and women who belong to the church (see also Eph. 1:22, 23; 4:12; 5:30; Col. 1:18). In studying the church of Jesus Christ, we do not find males to be superior to females. They are both ontologically the same, saved by the same grace of Christ, kept by the same grace, and answerable to Christ (1 Pet. 3:7). Both males and females constitute the same body of Christ of which He is the Head. Whereas there is no ontological superiority, there is a functional differentiation, and this is what the Apostle Paul is anxious to address in 1 Corinthians 11.

LESSONS:

1. In this passage, Paul is not intimating that a woman is inferior to a man in the marriage relationship, but that the husband has the functional responsibility of being the head of the Christian unit.
2. This verse cannot contradict what 1 Peter 3:7 states. The Word of God is not contradictory, but complementary.

3. The husband and wife are presented by Christ as one body, with the husband as the representative of the relationship. In this respect, he is said to be the head of the wife. He is the functional head, and the two must operate as if they are one, which is the only way to fulfill the purpose for which marriage was established.
4. Paul says that the head of Christ is God, meaning the Father, in order to illustrate that although there are two Persons, both are God, but each functions differently, just as the husband and the wife in Christian marriage.

1 Cor. 11:4 | *Men Who Pray with Covered Heads*

Every man praying or prophesying having his head covered brings shame to his head.

Corinth was a Greek city inhabited by Jews, Gentiles, and Christians. All three groups are mentioned in 1 Corinthians 10:32. At the time that Paul visited Corinth, distinctions between the genders and ethnic groups were prominent. The Jewish custom was for men to cover their heads in the synagogue while women did not. However, the Greek custom in the churches was the opposite, hence confusion prevailed because the church was made up of both converted Jews and Gentiles.

One of the questions that arose in the Christian church of Corinth was whether or not the Greek custom, the uncovering of the head of men and covering the head of women, should be followed or the opposite Jewish tradition.

Perhaps one lesson we can learn here is that it is not pleasing to the Lord to let our particular customs become bones of contention. The Jews were in the Greek city of Corinth and undoubtedly were a minority group in contrast to the Greeks who predominated. It is possible that they were trying to force their Jewish customs on the Greeks although they were fewer in number. In my travels and teaching around the world, I have encountered a great many customs which are different from my own. As much as possible, I try to adapt to the prevalent custom and not bring shame on the name of Christ by showing indifference to the convictions of those I am among.

This discussion in the eleventh chapter of 1 Corinthians is, in fact, a continuation of Paul's discussion concerning the unimportant things of life that had nothing to do with the all-important matter of salvation. It falls in the same category as eating foods sacrificed to idols. Apparently, this matter of a head covering was the cause of much contention among the believers in Corinth, and Paul is trying to correct the problem. We deduce this from verse 16 in which Paul states, "But if any man seem to be contentious [*philóneikos* {5380}, derived from *phílos* {5384}, a friend, and *neíkos*, not occurring in the NT by itself and meaning contention, dispute], we have no such custom, neither the churches of God."

In verse 3, Paul spoke about relationships. He spoke of a husband and wife in their marital relationship. They have Christ as their head. He spoke of the head of the wife being the husband, and he spoke of God the Father being the head of Christ in their eternal relationship. Paul maintains men and women are to keep the distinct characteristics of masculinity and femininity as they relate to each other in a married relationship.

"Every Man Praying"

Paul begins verse 4 with the masculine adjective *pás* (3956), all, every, and in verse 5 he uses *pása*, the feminine. He insists on the preservation of the genders. The word *anḗr* (435) is a man, a male; and in verse 6 he uses *gunḗ* (1135), a woman, a female. In these two verses he definitely distinguishes the genders, even though he does not speak only of a husband and wife. What he says, of course, extends also to husbands and wives, but it is applicable generally to both men and women.

Paul was interested especially in the proper function of men and women in the church. He believed that both had the right and duty to pray. This is why in both cases he says "praying" (*proseuchómenos* [masculine] and *proseuchoménē* [feminine], the nominative present middle deponent participial form of *proseúchomai* [4336], to pray) or "prophesying" (*prophēteúōn* [masculine] and *prophēteúousa* [feminine], the nominative singular present active participial form of *prophēteúō* [4395], to prophesy) are permissible. Of course, verse 4 is in the masculine, and verse 5 is in the feminine. The present participle implies **whenever** he or she prays. *Proseúchomai* is the most general word for prayer to God, for expressing one's wish (*euchḗ* [2171], wish).

The question that immediately arises is whether Paul is referring to public or private prayer. There is no doubt that he refers to public prayer in the company of men and women in the church or elsewhere.

"Or Prophesying"

The next word is *ḗ* (2228), "or." "Every man praying **or** prophesying [*prophēteúōn*, the nominative singular masculine present active participial form of *prophēteúō* {to prophesy}]." The word "prophesying" is made up of the preposition *pró* (4253), before or forth, and *phēmí* (5346), to tell. It means to foretell or tell forth. A prophecy is made in the presence of others and involves speaking. Since it is praying or prophesying, and prophesying involves telling, we must also interpret praying as utilizing the tongue in the presence of others to tell one's mind to God. There is no doubt that prophesying involves an audience (1 Cor. 13:9; 14:1, 3, 24, 31, 39). These two verses are the only verses in the New Testament in which both praying and prophesying are mentioned together in this respect.

"Having His Head Covered"

What has been rendered "having his head covered" is from the Greek *katá* (2596), down; *kephalḗs*, of the head, the genitive singular feminine noun of *kephalḗ* (2776), head; and *echōn*, the nominative singular masculine present active participial form of *échō* (2192), to have, having. This phrase *katá kephalḗs* occurs nowhere else in the New Testament. It does not say what the man is wearing on his head. Perhaps it may have been a covering or a hat resembling something a woman wore. The emphasis is that a man is different from a woman, and he must appear different.

"Brings Shame to His Head"

By covering his head, this man brings shame (*kataischúnei*, the third person singular present active indicative of *kataischúnō* [2617]) by having done something out of order. In verse 3, Paul has told us that the head of man is Christ. Therefore, Christ ought to be respected and not put to shame.

The covering of the head also may be interpreted as long hair which falls down over the head of the man (v. 7). The lesson is that a man should not look like a woman by growing long hair or by having any covering on his head that resembles something a woman would wear.

We can carry this a step further and say that any behavior that is shocking to society in general, and to the family of God in particular, brings shame to our Lord.

LESSONS:

1. Here the Apostle Paul uses the term "man" to refer to men in general, and not specifically to husbands.
2. Both in design and in appearance men and women are different, and it is sinful when either, in any way, attempts to look like the other gender.

3. Since a man symbolizes Christ, wrongful behavior brings shame to his head which is Christ.
4. We should not scoff at the customs of those whom we are among. This also brings shame to the name of Christ.

1 Cor. 11:5 | *Women Who Pray with Uncovered Heads*

> *But every woman praying or prophesying with her head uncovered brings shame on her head, and it is one and the same thing as if she had it shaven.*

This verse provides a contrast between males and females as worshipers in the church. Paul's main concern is that the males look like males and the females look like females.

"But Every Woman"

The verse begins with *pása*, the nominative singular feminine adjectival form of *pás* (3956), every. In Greek, adjectives as well as nouns have genders. Here the feminine is *pása* whereas the masculine is *pás*. All the participles agree with the gender, like *prophēteúousa*, a woman prophesying.

The contrast is provided with the adversative particle *dé* (1161), but. It distinguishes the difference between every man and every woman. No exceptions are made.

The word for "woman" is *gunḗ* (1135) which here means basically a woman, but by extension it can mean a wife.

"Praying or Prophesying"

A woman, therefore, is presented as praying or prophesying. Both participles are in the feminine nominative form. It is exactly the same that a male, and by extension a husband, does in church. This is in answer to the question as to whether a woman can pray or prophesy in church. The indisputable answer is yes. However, we must examine in detail what praying or prophesying involves. This passage of Scripture is the only one in which the two words are equated. Note that it does not say "and" prophesying, but "or" (*ḗ* [2228]) prophesying.

The assemblies of believers in the apostolic age consisted of both men and women as today. We find at the first prayer meeting held in an upper room in Jerusalem (Acts 1:12–14) that "these [the disciples] all continued with one accord in prayer and supplication, with the women and Mary the mother of Jesus, and with His brothers." A definite distinction is made here between the men who were present and the women. Was their prayer public or private? If it were private, it would indicate that each one prayed silently, but when they were gathered together and were praying, we can safely conclude that they were audibly praying in obedience to the command of Jesus Christ, now risen from the dead. A great event consequent to His resurrection was the baptism in the Holy Spirit (Acts 1:5, 6). There was no distinction between men and women in this. Therefore, it is inconceivable that this was silent prayer, although it is not clearly stated whether or not the women who were present participated in the audible praying in any way.

In Acts 12:5–19, we find that Peter is in jail in Jerusalem. A prayer meeting was held in the home of Mary, the mother of John Mark. When a knock was heard at the door, a young girl (*paidískē* [3814]) answered. She and Mary were the two females whom we know were part of the meeting. It is very unlikely that the prayers offered at that meeting were not audible. And it is also most unlikely that Mary, in whose house the prayer meeting was held and for whom the imprisonment of Peter was of great interest, would not participate in the prayer.

In Acts 16:13–15, near a river outside Philippi, Lydia was a member of a group of women at prayer. Undoubtedly, this was public, audible prayer in which the women participated.

In Acts 18:2, 3; Romans 16:3; 1 Corinthians 16:19, and 2 Timothy 4:19, we have reference to a married couple called Priscilla and Aquilla. These verses suggest that this couple was precious to Paul. The man was a Jew (Acts 18:2), but Priscilla, his wife, was not a Jewess. Because her name is usually put first, we are led to believe that she may have been of a higher social standing or education than her husband. Perhaps she was a member of some distinguished Roman family. It is believed that she was a Roman who was saved and became a missionary. They both came from Italy to Corinth "Because Claudius had commanded all the Jews to depart from Rome" (Acts 18:2). Priscilla accompanied her Jewish husband to Corinth where they followed their trade as tentmakers. Their house became a meeting place for the church, both in Ephesus and Rome. Paul, who also pursued the tentmaking vocation, greatly influenced them to become earnest Christians and enthusiastic helpers. Writing to the Corinthian church in later years, the Apostle says, "Aquilla and Priscilla greet you much in the Lord" (1 Cor. 16:19).

When Paul went to Ephesus, Priscilla and Aquilla went with him and remained there to work while he visited Jerusalem. So the initial work in Ephesus was done by Priscilla and Aquilla. They tried to prepare the ground before Paul returned and to sow the seed of Christian teaching as far as they were able. During this time, Apollos came to Ephesus with his imperfect apprehension of Christianity. Aquilla and Priscilla admired his learning and his earnestness; and, recognizing that such a man must either be a strong supporter of the cause or an influential opponent, they were diligent to instruct him very carefully (Acts 18:26). The Scriptures tell us that both of them taught him. Here is a couple, man and woman, teaching a man. Subsequent events throw doubt on the ability of this couple, who were themselves recent converts, to educate the eloquent Alexandrian in the Pauline interpretation of the gospel. Nevertheless, Priscilla and Aquilla seemed to have fulfilled their mission with skill and courage; and, when a church was gathered, the members met in their house (1 Cor. 16:19). The Apostle Paul did not in any way distinguish between this couple as to their genders. His description of them was, "My fellow workers in Christ Jesus who for my life laid down their own necks; unto whom not only I give thanks, but also all the churches of the Gentiles" (Rom. 16:3, 4). This sets them side by side with the Apostle. Paul calls both of them his coworkers. They labored along with him in a preeminent manner, and the Scriptures have attested to their worth as independent workers (cf. J. E. Roberts in James Hastings's *Dictionary of the Apostolic Church,* Vol. 1, pp. 87, 88).

In Philippians 4:2, 3 Paul recognizes two women by the names of Euodía and Suntúchē as fellow workers of his who needed help. He calls them "those women which labored with me in the gospel." The question arises as to how they could have labored with him without doing any public speaking. There is no doubt that women labored together with the men. They could not have been silent laborers.

A woman by the name of Chloe and her household were very active in the church of Corinth, and they became informants of its true condition for Paul (1 Cor. 1:11). In the greetings that Paul gives to the church of Rome in Romans 16, he includes several women (Phoebe [v. 1], Priscilla with her husband Aquilla [v. 3], Tryphaena and Tryphosa [v. 12], Persis [v. 12], and Julia [v. 15]).

"With Her Head Uncovered"

First Corinthians 11:5 teaches that a woman can both pray and prophesy in a public service; however, it should not be done with her head uncovered.

Now what does the word "uncovered" mean? It means without the natural covering of the hair or without an artificial covering in the form of a hat. The word "uncovered" is *akatakalúptō*, the dative singular feminine adjectival form of *akatakáluptos* (177) derived from the privative *alpha* or *a* (1), without; the preposition *katá* (2596), down, an intensive; and *kalúptō* (2572), to cover. In verse 6, Paul speaks of the covering of the head either being a woman's hair, as God gave it, or if she happened to have it shaven, an artificial cover in the form of a hat or veil. We must not forget that the main thesis of the Apostle Paul is that there should be a distinction between a male and a female insofar as their appearance was concerned. Indecent men grew their hair long, which hung down from their heads. Indecent women cut their hair short, and this, according to some, was a clear demonstration that they belonged to the class of prostitutes. There must have been instances when some women were saved who had their hair shaven, indicating they had lived a life of sin (1 Cor. 6:9–11). The first thing that a new believer is urged to do is to exercise the access that he has to God in faith (Rom. 5:1–3). He must pray to God and thank Him for the work of Christ in his heart, and he must open his mouth to tell God's great work of salvation in his life. However, it takes time for hair to grow. Between the time of salvation and the natural time that it takes for the hair to grow, must a woman not pray and tell of the grace of God in her life? Paul says she must, but with her head covered. Since she has to wait for the natural covering of hair to grow, she can do these things in the meantime with an artificial covering or hat. This is what the Apostle Paul means when he speaks of covering the head while one prays and prophesies.

"Brings Shame on Her Head"

If the woman, who is saved, prays in public and speaks of the grace of God without her hair having grown or having her head covered artificially, she brings shame on her head. The verb "brings shame" is *kataischúnei* (the third person singular present active indicative of *kataischúnō* [2617], brings shame), exactly the same verb as we find in verse 4.

The shame is brought upon her own head (*heautḗs*, the genitive singular feminine third person reflexive pronoun *heautoú* [1438], his, but used here as emphatic). In verse 3, Paul told us that the head of a married woman is her husband. Probably the saved woman in this verse does not have a husband, since most of these women were prostitutes. Therefore, she brings shame on her own head. In what way? With her mouth she prays and prophesies or tells of the grace of God. In other words, she gives her testimony. But her appearance, having her head uncovered, does not agree with her testimony. Her appearance portrays her as still being a prostitute and not having been sanctified by Christ. It is a great shame to the gospel to say one thing and yet behave in another manner, to claim salvation and to continue in the lifestyle of a sinner. Looking and behaving like nonbelievers is shameful. Christians should appear as decent and respectable.

"And It Is One and the Same Thing as if She Had It Shaven"

The teaching of the Apostle Paul is that outward appearance must give testimony to the reality of the inner transformation. There are two Greek words used in the New Testament which make that clear. One, occurring in 1 Corinthians 4:6, 2 Corinthians 11:13–15, and Philippians 3:21, is the word *metaschēmatízo* (3345) and means to transform one's outer appearance. The other word, occurring in Romans 12:2 and 2 Corinthians 3:18, refers to an inner change. It is *metamorphóomai* (3339). Paul's teaches that if these women were going to appear with their heads uncovered when they prayed and prophesied, it would be an indication they were still prostitutes.

When Paul states in verse 5 that a woman can pray and prophesy in testimony of her conversion as long as she has her head covered, either naturally or artificially, does he contradict what he says in 1 Corinthians 14:33–35? We have stated that *anḗr* (435) can mean either a man or a husband, and *gunḗ* can mean a woman or a wife. While in 1 Corinthians 11:4, 5 the two words mean a man and a woman, that is, a male and female, in 1 Corinthians 14:33–35, the terms mean a husband and wife. Let us briefly study these verses. "For God is not the author of confusion [*akatastasías*, the genitive singular feminine noun of *akatastasía* {181}, confusion, instability, commotion, derived from the privative *alpha* or *a*; and *katástasis*, which is not found in the NT but means the prevailing condition of order]." There was a certain order that prevailed in the churches. Nothing should be done that would detract from the message being given by the one preaching. Verse 34 should not read, "Let your **women**," but "Let your **wives** in the churches maintain silence [*sigā́tōsan*, the third person plural present active imperative of *sigáō* {4601}, to keep silence]." This implies that they should keep silent if their speaking causes a commotion or a disturbance of the order that should prevail. Now the seating order in a church was that the men usually sat together in the front or downstairs, and the women sat in a separate section, perhaps in the balcony. Since there was no sound system such as we have today and if the women could not hear well, they would ask their husbands what was said. This, of course, would prove disruptive. Thus the Apostle Paul clearly recommends that a wife ask her husband to repeat or to discuss such things with her at home. Clearly the church was not the place to pose such questions, and it would create a great deal of commotion if the wives called to their husbands in other areas of the church.

The command that follows should never be taken in isolation, but in the context in which it was given. "For it is not permitted unto them [the wives] to speak." This word "speak" is the Greek verb *laleín*, the present active infinitive of *laléō* (2980). It is used consistently in the discussion of Paul regarding speaking in an unknown tongue, and in this context, to speak devoid of thought. Anyone who would loudly ask her husband, or anybody else for that matter, any question about anything while in church and disturb the order of the church service, would certainly not be using proper judgment.

"But they are commanded to be under obedience." This is a very poor translation of the verb *hupotássomai* (5293). It actually means to place oneself in order under, which wives are to do in relation to their husbands (Eph. 5:22; Col. 3:18; Titus 2:5; 1 Pet. 3:1, 5).

And verse 35 says, "And if they [the wives] want to learn anything, let them ask [*eperōtátōsan*, the third person plural present active imperative of *eperōtáō* {1905}, to interrogate, derived from *epí* {1909}, an intensive meaning 'upon,' and *erōtáō* {2065}, to ask, inquire, let them make specific inquiry] their husbands." The translators correctly used the plural accusative of *anḗr* here as meaning husband. Then follows a general statement which again has been poorly translated: "For it is a shame for women to speak in the church." This should be "For it is a shame for wives to speak in church [in the context of causing commotion, confusion, and disruption in the order of the church]." It does not say in any way that it is forbidden for women to speak in church, but rather implies that wives are to question their husbands after the service. These wives were advised to wait until they were home to ask their husbands whatever was on their minds.

The other passage which seems to contradict the thought that a woman is forbidden to speak in church is 1 Timothy 2:11, 12. Again, it is a matter of understanding the words that are used. The word *gunḗ* here means "wife." The verse should read, "Let the wife learn in silence with all subordination [*hupotagḗ* {5292}, subordination, a verb that is derived from *hupotássomai*, to place oneself under in an orderly fashion, which is the same verb used for wives submitting themselves to their husbands]." For a woman to submit herself to men in general would be contrary to the teaching of the Word of God. The Word of God teaches the wives to be submissive to their own husbands, not to any and every man. Then verse 12 says, "But I do not permit a wife to teach" (a.t.). Here *gunaikí*, the dative singular feminine noun of *gunḗ*, "a wife," should not be translated "a woman," because there are many women who are teachers. Paul does not object to the women teaching, but to the wives teaching in church in the presence of their husbands. Paul explains why this kind of teaching should not occur—it may lead the wife to usurp authority over her husband. What is translated as "usurp authority" is *authenteín*, the present active infinitive of *authentéō* (831). This is derived from the noun *authéntēs* (not found in the NT) and meaning a murderer, an absolute master, which in turn comes from *autós* (846), himself, and *éntea* (again not found in the NT), and means arms or armor. The noun means a self-appointed killer with one's own hand, one acting by his own authority or power. A wife teaching her husband causes her to believe that she knows more than her husband and may lead her to become authoritarian, which contradicts the scriptural teaching that a wife should submit to her husband (Eph. 5:22; Col. 3:18). The verse closes with Paul's instruction that the wife should learn and be "in quietness [*en* {1722}, in; *hēsuchía* {2271}, quiet, tranquility]," and not "in silence" as expressed by the translators. If the word were "silence," it would have been the noun *sigḗ* (4602), silence. So the Apostle Paul instructs that in church a wife should not teach her husband, because that would lead to an authoritarian attitude which would disrupt the pattern set by God.

LESSONS:

1. We can ascertain that the word *gunḗ* (1135) here means "woman" and not "wife," for otherwise it would imply that only wives are permitted to pray. This would provide an unacceptable limitation to the universal privilege of a believer to pray, whether male or female (Rom. 5:2; Gal. 3:28).
2. The restriction concerns the appearance of a woman versus her expression of prayer or prophecy (1 Tim. 3:11).
3. If a woman was saved from the ranks of the prostitutes having her head shaven, she should not wait until her hair grew naturally to demonstrate that she was no more a prostitute, but a child of God. In such a case, the only way to cover her shaven head would be to use an artificial covering.
4. Verse 4 teaches that a man should not have long hair covering his head whereas a woman should. In case she was shaven, she should wear a hat or veil.

1 Cor. 11:6 | A Safeguard against Shame

For if a woman be not covered, let her also be shorn. But since it is shameful for a woman to be shorn, let her cover herself.

From the context, we conclude that it is an honorable thing for a woman to have her hair long and thereby have her head covered.

"For if a Woman Be Not Covered, Let Her Also Be Shorn"

Our verse, which poses an irony, begins with the subjective conjunction *ei* (1487), if, suppose. The "not" is the absolute negative *ou* (3756). The verb that is used is *katakalúptetai*, the third person singular present middle/passive indicative of *katakalúptō* (2619), to cover completely, derived from the preposition *katá* (2596), an intensive meaning down, and *kalúptō* (2572), to cover. It means to cover with a veil or something which hangs down. The verb is used only in verses 6 and 7 of this chapter. The word with the opposite meaning is *akatakáluptos* (177), unveiled or not completely covered, and it occurs in verses 5 and 13. If the woman refuses to be covered, then let her be shorn (*keirásthō,* the third person singular aorist middle imperative of *keírō* [2751], to cut the hair short) and bear her shame.

"But Since *It Is* Shameful for a Woman to Be Shorn, Let Her Cover Herself"

The next sentence also begins with the conjunction *ei.* However, here, as in many instances, it involves not a subjective supposition, but a certainty and should be translated "since" as in Matthew 19:10; Acts 5:39; Philippians 2:1, etc. It was certainly shameful for a Christian woman in Corinth to have her hair short or shaven (*xurásthai*, the present middle/passive infinitive of *xuráō* [3587], to shave), and since it was a shame, she should be covered or veiled (*katakaluptésthō*, the third person singular present middle imperative of *katakalúptō*, to cover completely or to veil.) So veiling or covering the head was mandated for women who had short hair or a shaven head.

Covering her head was the only honorable thing for a woman to do to hide the shame of having short hair or a shaven head which indicated a previous immoral lifestyle (1 Cor. 6:10–11).

LESSONS:

1. Since the custom was to consider any woman with short hair or a shaven head, for whatever reason, shameful, she should cover her head.
2. If any woman with short hair or a shaven head refused to cover her head, then she brought shame to herself and to Christ.
3. The believer should do nothing that would bring shame on the name of Christ.

1 Cor. 11:7 | *Why Men Should Not Cover Their Heads*

For, on the one hand, a man does not have to cover his head being the image and glory of God; on the other hand, the woman is the glory of man.

Paul now discusses a covering for the head of a man and gives us the reason a man should not cover his head.

"For, on the One Hand, a Man Does Not Have to Cover His Head"

There are two particles found in this verse which do not necessarily appear in the translation. One is *mén* (3303) which we translated "on the one hand," and which affirms and points out something different that is to follow. The other particle is *dé* (1161) which we translated as "on the other hand." On the one hand, we have man who does not need to cover his head, and this is based on the supposition that the woman is instructed to cover hers. "Does not have to" is expressed with the verb *ouk opheílei*, the third person singular present active indicative of *opheílō* (3784), to be obligated, to perform a duty, meaning ought to, must, and it is followed by the verb *katakalúptesthai*, the present middle infinitive of *katakalúptō* (2619), to completely cover or fall down from the head. In contrast to the woman who has to cover her head, it is not necessary for the man to do so.

"Being the Image and Glory of God"

Paul now tells us why man does not have to cover his head: "being the image and glory of God." "Being" translates *hupárchōn*, the nominative singular masculine present active participle of *hupárchō* (5225), to exist originally. The meaning of this participle does not only indicate what man is now, but what he had been originally (Phil. 2:6). Man, the male, from the beginning has been the image (*eikṓn* [1504]) and glory (*dóxa* [1391]) of God. The word *eikṓn*, image, always assumes a prototype. Man, especially the male, was created in the image and likeness of God (Gen. 1:26). Genesis 1:27 tells us that the male and female were created by God, and in Genesis 2:21–25, we are told that the woman was formed from the man's rib. The noun *dóxa*, glory, is derived from the verb *dokéō* (1380), to think, consider, appear, recognize. So man, being the image of God, also is the glory of the true recognition of God.

The noun "God" (*Theoú*, the genitive singular masculine noun of *Theós* [2316], God) does not have the definite article *toú* (3588), the, in front of it. The intimation here is that God is referred to in His eternal, infinite, essential existence, which is Spirit (John 4:24). No distinction is made to a particular Personality within the Deity. Man, when he was created, was created in the image and likeness of God. But God was one Person in three, Father, Son, and Holy Spirit (Matt. 28:19). This is what Jesus Christ came to reveal to us when He became incarnate. Genesis 1:26 says, "And God said, 'Let **us** make man in **our** image after **our** likeness.'" It was only one image, the image of the Triune God.

"The Woman Is the Glory of Man"

The woman or female is contrasted to the man, the male. The contrast, as we said at the beginning of our study, is demonstrated by the two particles, *mén*, "on the one hand" mentioned in regard to man, and *dé*, "on the other hand," mentioned in regard to the woman. "The woman [*gunḗ*] is [*estin*, the third person singular present indicative of *eimí* {1510}, to be, is] the glory [*dóxa* of the man; *andrós*, the genitive singular masculine noun of *anḗr* {435}, man]." Thus the woman is the true recognition of the man. Generally speaking, when we see whom a man has chosen for his wife, we will understand what he is.

In the detailed story of creation, although God created man, or humanity, in His image, nevertheless He is specifically the creator of both male and female (Gen. 1:27), although He fashioned the woman out of the man (Gen. 2:21–23). He used the male to make the female.

Why does the Apostle use the two verbs *hupárchō,* being, and *estín,* is, when he says that man does not need to cover his head? The verb "being" is used when he speaks of man being the image and glory of God, but the verb "is" is used when he says that the woman is the glory of the man. The woman was not created as the image and glory of God from the beginning, as was the man. The word *hupárchōn,* being, implies the beginning. The woman was not from the beginning of creation, but she is now existent. This verse declares that man originally was the image and glory of God; however, he fell. When the Genesis passage speaks of the woman though, it does not say this. The Word of God does not tell us what she **was**, but what she now **is**. She is her husband's pride and joy in which he brags and glories. In a healthy marriage relationship as God designed it, the husband finds happiness and pleasure in his wife. He is proud to have people know that she is his and his alone. The noun *gunḗ* in this verse has the double meaning of a woman and a wife.

In Corinth, the woman who refused to have her head covered showed that she was living in sin and was not ashamed of it. Remember that only prostitutes in Corinth had short hair or were shaven for easy recognition of their lewd lifestyle. Any man who chose such a woman for his companion showed what he really was, an immoral man. This is what the last statement in this verse means. *Dóxa* really is better translated "reputation" instead of "glory," for "glory" in English rarely has an evil connotation. Here, however, Paul uses the word *dóxa*, first in a good sense, referring to the glory of God or the recognition of God for what He really is, and then in thc evil sense when it refers to man who keeps company with a prostitute. The company that a man keeps reveals his character.

LESSONS:

1. Men do not need to have their heads covered when praying.
2. The husband should love his wife and take pride in her.
3. An uncovered head for a woman in Corinth was a sign of an immoral lifestyle.
4. When a man keeps company with a woman who has a bad reputation, it reveals his character.

1 Cor. 11:8 | *God Created Woman Out of Man*

For man is not out of a woman, but the woman out of man.

Paul did not believe in the evolution of the sexes, but accepted the sexes in their constituent form and shape as made by God. He believed in the uniqueness of the human race consisting of man and woman. Their differences, however, are valid and need to be maintained.

"For Man Is Not Out of a Woman"

In this verse, Paul states the case as it is. The case involves absolute principles. It explains why man is the head of the woman (v. 3). He is not superior to his wife because both have experienced the work of redemption by Christ (Gal. 3:28; 1 Pet. 3:7).

Both man and woman, especially in marriage, ought to recognize that there is no independence under God. The man is dependent upon Christ, and although the woman is dependent upon Christ too (1 Pet. 3:7), she is also dependent upon her husband, and they are made into one body because of Christ (Matt. 19:5; Mark 10:8; Eph. 5:31).

This verse is an explanation of what Paul propounded in the previous verses, that the husband is the head of the wife in a God-approved marital relationship. The verse begins with the absolute negative *ou* (3756), not, and *gár* (1063), therefore: "For man is absolutely not out of a woman." In verse 12, there are two prepositions used although the translation may indicate that the same preposition is used regarding a woman and a man. The correct translation is, "For as the woman is of [*ek* {1537}, out of] the man, thus also the man through [*diá* {1223}], the woman, but all out of [*ek*] God." No man was ever born of a woman without the help and input of man, except Jesus Christ, who was born of a virgin without the activity of a man. Jesus constituted a unique male who became a man of His own volition.

Galatians 4:4 speaks of Jesus in His incarnation as having been made (*genómenon*, the accusative singular masculine second aorist middle deponent participial form of *gínomai* [1096], to become) out of a woman. The expression is *ek*, out of, and *gunaikos*, the genitive singular feminine noun of *gunḗ* (1135), woman. "Out of a woman" is exactly the same phrase we find in 1 Corinthians 11:8. Jesus Christ, in His human birth, constituted an exception in that He did not come out of the joining together of a man with a woman, but simply "out of a woman" alone, because He was born of a virgin who conceived through the Holy Spirit (Luke 1:26–37). Jesus was not merely man, but He was the God-Man. Every other man, however, is born of a woman, but with the necessary activity of the sperm of a man.

"But the Woman Out of Man"

Thus Paul says, "But woman out of man [*ek,* which because the next word begins with a vowel, becomes *ex*; *andrós*, the genitive singular masculine noun of *anḗr* {435}, man]." Here he speaks of the absolute involvement of the male with the female to produce another human being.

LESSONS:

1. Paul views humanity as the specific creation of God.
2. Absolutely no woman can produce children without the activity of man.
3. Man takes the initiative; therefore, there can be no propagation of the human race without his contribution to the reproductive act.

1 Cor. 11:9 | *God Made the Woman for the Man*

Furthermore, man was not made for the woman, but woman for the man.

In the previous verse Paul states things as they are in regard to the form and shape of a man and a woman. They did not evolve into what they are, but they are what they are as a result of the creative act of God.

"Furthermore, Man Was Not Made for the Woman, but the Woman for the Man"

The mind of Paul is taken especially by the relationship that God wanted to establish between one man and one woman in the wonderful and God-ordained bond of marriage. This is shown by the construction of the sentences: "Man [*anḗr* {435} without the article] was not made for [*diá* {1223}, for, meaning for the purpose of] **the** woman." The same is true of the contrasting sentence: "But woman for **the** [*diá tón*, the definite article] man [or husband]." God made man for **the** woman and woman for **the** man. This is definitely a declaration against homosexuality and an affirmation of heterosexuality and monogamy, one man for **the** woman and one woman for **the** man. The verb that is used in this verse is *ektísthē*, the third person singular aorist passive indicative of *ktizō* (2936), to create, produce, to form out of preexistent matter. The aorist tense indicates a particular time that God created man. *Ktízō* has in it an intellectual and volitional process. It is the most commonly used New Testament verb to indicate the creative act of God.

Although God created man in His own image, He formed male and female. In the detailed account of how the woman was formed, we read that God caused a deep sleep to fall upon Adam, "and he slept; and He took one of his ribs, and closed up the flesh instead thereof (Gen. 2:21)." I can hear the atheists of many years ago ridiculing this portion of Scripture. How could anybody be so sound asleep that someone could open him up and remove one of his ribs and then close it up again? This is impossible, the unbeliever would say. But we stand in awe today when we consider the wonderful things that are done in surgery—and the person is sound asleep and cannot remember anything about it afterwards. "And the rib which the Lord God had taken from man, made He a woman, and brought her unto the man. And Adam said, 'This is now bone of my bones, and flesh of my flesh: she shall be called woman, because she was taken out of man' " (Gen. 2:22–23, cf. 1:26, 27). There is no doubt that at a certain time God formed woman out of man, and thus Paul could say, "Furthermore, man was not made for the woman, but woman for the man."

The preposition *diá*, for, is used with the accusative, which sometimes means "because of" or "due to." Here *diá* means a definitive purpose that is exclusive. God made it that way, and we would be foolish to resist God's wisdom. We must never forget that, in using the words "man" (*anḗr*) and "woman" (*gunḗ* [1135]), Paul does not exclusively have in mind the male and female genders, but that God made specifically a woman to be a man's wife, and, while she is equal in the Lord's sight, He made the husband to be her head.

LESSONS:

1. God created male and female in His image (Gen. 1:27).
2. God specifically created a wife for Adam by taking out one of his ribs and forming a woman.
3. God is all-wise, and it is foolish and contemptible to resist His wisdom.

1 Cor. 11:10 | Angels Are Watching

For this reason a woman ought to exercise authority over her head because of the angels.

Verse 8 states the fact that without the activity of man there can be no woman or any other human being. Verse 9 states that this is so because God made it that way. First, He created man and then, from his rib, He made a woman to be the man's wife. No matter how intelligent and educated we become, we cannot change our sexuality. The surgeons sometimes try, but they never end with a true member of the opposite sex, merely a mutilated individual. God made us as male and female, and there cannot be a perpetuation of the human race without the participation of the man and the bringing forth by woman.

But it is a privilege and advantage for a woman to place herself under the care and protection of her husband. We saw that this is expressed by the verb *hupotássomai* (5293), to place oneself under in one's proper order (Eph. 5:22; Col. 3:18–21; Titus 2:4–8; 1 Pet. 3:1–7). This is by volition on the woman's part and obedience to the order which God has set. When it comes to children (Eph. 6:1; Col. 3:20), the verb that is used is *hupakoúō* (5219), to obey, although not necessarily with consent, for children may rebel because they do not know what is best for them.

This is also the verb that is used in the case of the wind (Matt. 8:27) and the unclean spirits obeying Christ (Mark 1:27).

"For This Reason a Woman Ought to Exercise Authority over Her Head"

"For this reason" refers to the two previous verses. The verb "ought to" is *opheílei*, the third person singular present active indicative of *opheílō* (3784), to owe, to be indebted, to be morally obligated. It is the second time in this chapter that this verb occurs in the present indicative which indicates continuity of obligation. The first occurrence is in verse 7 where it is stated that man must not cover his head. This constitutes his moral obligation, especially when he is a believer. Now Paul speaks of the moral obligation of a woman who is also a believer. She ought to exercise authority over her own head. This word "head" here does not refer to rank of authority and responsibility as does verse 3. It rather means that it is within the woman's own moral prerogative to cover or not to cover her head. Paul does not say that she must cover her head, but that she must exercise this authority herself. In other words, this constitutes a voluntary act consequent to the realization that God made her out of the man and for the man, that is, for her husband in particular. This word "authority" comes from the Greek *exousía* (1849), right, authority (see 1 Cor. 8:9; 9:4–6, 12, 18), and the verb *éxestin* (1832), it is permissible (see 1 Cor. 6:12; 10:23).

The word "authority" goes perfectly well with the use of the verb *hupotássomai*, to place oneself under, which is required in relation to her husband. She should not obey (*hupakoúō*) without the exercise of thought, as children are supposed to do in respect to their parents. The woman, and particularly a wife, has the authority, the right, or prerogative to cover her head or not to do so. If she does so, it is a demonstration that she follows God's design and order. This privilege has been given to her by God because she, along with man, has been created in His image. The verb *opheílei*, ought to, is followed by the word *échein*, the present active infinitive of *échō* (2192), to have, which in this case relates to the innate authority which a woman has, and Paul realizes that she has it also as a result of being one of God's creations. However, when it comes to the marital relationship, she ought to voluntarily submit the authority she has from God in accordance with His design, that is, to her husband, and place herself in perfect arrangement for a happy marital life. Any woman, when married, ought to submit the authority she has over her head to her husband. How she treats her head, either with long hair or a covering, declares her attitude toward her husband. What she does with this authority has a moral consequence.

"Because of the Angels"

A woman ought to exercise authority over her head "for the angels." This is translated from *diá* (1223), for; *toús*, the accusative plural masculine article of *ho* (3588), the; and *aggélous*, the accusative plural masculine noun of *ággelos* (32), angel.

Who are the angels? Hebrews 1:14 tells us: "Are they not all ministering spirits, sent forth to minister for them who shall be heirs of salvation?" In 1 Corinthians 4:9, the Apostle tells us that we, as believers, "are made a spectacle unto the world, and to angels, and to men." In other words, we are watched over by the angels as we endure and suffer for God. Here, in 1 Corinthians 11:10, Paul tells us that the angels are watching to see whether Christian women exhibit the proper authority over their heads by covering them in demonstration that they are obedient to God and His Word; and although they are equal with men, they are subservient to their own husbands. The preposition *diá* with the accusative shows both cause and purpose (Rom. 4:25). Because the angels are watching the women, it is necessary that they not be offensive.

LESSONS:

1. A woman is not required to submit unwillingly to her husband. She does so because she willingly chooses to do so. This is demonstrated by the verb *hupotássomai* (5293), which means voluntary submission. If it is not voluntary, it is not the free exercise of her will.
2. Angels look down upon our behavior to see whether we rightly exercise our authority in Christ.

1 Cor. 11:11 | *Husbands and Wives as Indispensable Partners*

Nevertheless, neither is the man without the woman, nor the woman without the man in the Lord.

Paul is explaining the state of both men and women when they are attached to the Lord (1 Cor. 12:13). They are not independent of each other, because they are both members of the same body (Eph. 1:22, 23). The same work that the Lord does for a man, He also does for a woman in making her a member of the body of Christ.

"Nevertheless"

This verse begins with the adverb *plḗn* (4133) meaning much more or nevertheless. This emphasizes the underlying principle of the relationship between a man and a woman being "in the Lord." It is the only time Paul uses this word in his two Corinthian epistles as if he is stressing that being in the Lord is the most important basis of every relationship that exists between a man and woman. Paul has explained that a woman and a man are, for instance, at equal proximity to God, but they are formed differently. Both are human beings who have the same access to Him. However, we cannot disregard the fact that God made them differently in emotional make-up and appearance. What a loss it would be to humankind if we had not been created with the love and complementary factors found in the genders of a godly union of husband and wife. In the present discussion, Paul has brought out that although they both have basically the same kind of hair, each one can use it to demonstrate his or her gender. God has designed the sexuality of men and women to be apparent to others. Trying to hide the sexuality of either gender places that person in rebellion against his Creator. Man and woman stand on the opposite ends of a triangle. From each one, a line extends upward forming the apex of the triangle, which is God the Lord, and on whose absolute sovereignty everything depends, including the relationship of husband and wife with each other as they reach toward the apex.

The only place in Ephesians that *plḗn*, nevertheless, occurs is in 5:33 where Paul speaks of the believers being members of the body of Christ (v. 30) and of marriage as becoming one flesh (v. 31). Then he tells us in verse 32 that this is a mystery which applies to Christ and His church. Paul sums up his discourse with a basic absolute statement of fact which he introduces with "nevertheless":

> Nevertheless, let every one of you in particular, so love [*agapátō*, the third person singular present active imperative of *agapáō* {25}, to love] his wife even as himself; and the wife see that she reverence [*phobḗtai*, the third person singular present middle deponent subjunctive of *phobéō* {5399}, to fear, respect] her husband.

The continuous, sacrificial love of the husband toward his wife, such as he would naturally show for himself, creates in her a loving respect in return. This, however, presupposes Christ having performed the mystery of a godly union and maintaining it intact, as the present imperative would indicate.

The only other passages in which Paul uses *plḗn*, nevertheless, are Philippians 1:18; 3:16; 4:14.

"Neither Is the Man Without the Woman . . ."

The next word in our verse is *oúte* (3777) which we have translated as "neither," and which is derived from the absolute negative *ou* (3756), and the enclitic *te* (5037), and. The translation can be "neither," "nor," "not even," and "not" or "also not," referring usually to a part of a proposition. This conjunction (*oúte*) is repeated when Paul speaks of the woman: "nor the woman without the man." In verse 3, Paul told us that the head of every woman (wife) is the man (husband). In verse 7, he told us that the man should not have his head covered. But in verse 11, he wants us to realize that although the man (husband) is the head of the wife and should not cover his head, he cannot be independent. He absolutely must love his wife "in the Lord." His life would be nonperpetuating and, to a certain extent, unfulfilled without his wife. Paul does not want us to misunderstand his teachings about husbands as meaning that they can live their lives independent of their wives. Both the man and his wife are fully dependent upon each other, as they are both dependent upon the Lord.

The other word that attracts our attention in this verse is the word "without" (*chōrís* [5565], an adverb which means separately, by itself, apart). Paul speaks of a man and a woman, and particularly of a husband and wife, complementing each other in the Lord as He has so designed. It is not a man with a man because that would be a homosexual relationship, nor a woman with a woman, which is lesbianism. Such relationships are utterly condemned in the Scriptures. We must not forget what Paul said in 1 Corinthians 6:9–11. For any relationship or marriage to be blessed by God, it must be "in the Lord."

"In the Lord"

The phrase "in the Lord" is *en* (1722), in; *Kuríō*, the dative singular masculine noun of *Kúrios* (2962), Lord. There can be no independence of man from woman or woman from man, especially in the bond of marriage. If they belong to Christ, they belong to each other. They are interdependent because they are both dependent upon the Lord. Without women, men would cease to exist; and without men, women would cease to exist.

When God created the man, He said that it was not good for him to be alone (Gen. 2:18), so He made a counterpart for the man. As far as the man's counterpart was concerned, God said concerning her that her desire would be toward her husband (Gen. 3:16). It is the natural instinct of a woman to want to have and care for a home and a family. The husband's normal desire is to love and protect and provide for his wife and family, whereas she in turn loves and cares for him and the children—a perfect union "in the Lord."

We must stress here also that the marriage of a Christian is to be "**in** the Lord," that is, a believer should not marry an unbeliever, for if the couple is not "in the Lord," the hope of a happy marriage is slim indeed.

LESSONS:

1. Life for both a male and a female takes a different meaning when both husband and wife are "in the Lord."
2. In Christ, there is equality between the sexes, but there is also interdependence, one needing the other.
3. God created man and woman in such a way that they would complement each other.
4. Believers should marry only fellow believers which provides the best hope for a happy marriage.

1 Cor. 11:12 — *Man and Woman Are of God*

For indeed, as the woman is out of the man, thus also is the man through the woman, but all are out of God.

Remember how God created the woman out of the man? Now, through the woman, all people are brought into the world, but we must acknowledge that all come from God.

"For Indeed, as the Woman *Is* out of the Man, Thus Also *Is* the Man through the Woman"

In Greek, this verse begins with the adverb *hṓsper* (5618), as indeed, derived from *hōs* (5613), as, and the particle *per* (4007), indeed, which is contrasted with the adverb *hoútō* (3779), thus; and then followed by *gár* (1063), for, therefore. Paul refers to the original creative act of God and also to the reproductive system in human beings. He undoubtedly refers to Eve being created by God using the rib of Adam (Gen. 2:21–23). We find two important prepositions in this verse. The first is *ek* (1537), out of. The woman is said to come out of the man, Adam. The other preposition is *diá* (1223), through, in the phrase, "So *is* the man through the woman." God designed mankind to come into the world through the woman.

"But All *Are* Out of God"

For the second time, the preposition *ek*, out of, is used in reference to God's direct creative act: "But they all *are* out of God [*dé* {1161}, but; *tá*, the accusative plural neuter article of *ho* {3588}, the; *pánta*, the accusative plural neuter adjectival form of *pás* {3956}, all; *ek*, out of; *Theós* {2316}, God]." It makes no difference whether God created man from the dust of the earth or the woman from the man. The fact remains that He did. The adjective *pánta*, all, is an all-inclusive word which means every particular thing within the totality. Each kind and all kinds of created things and beings were made by God. Did you ever notice the word "kind" in the creation account in Genesis 1:11? The text reads "And God said, 'Let the earth bring forth grass, the herb yielding seed, and the fruit tree yielding fruit **after his kind**, whose seed is in itself, upon the earth': and it was so"! The phrase "after his kind" also occurs in verses 12, 21, 24, and 25, and then again in Genesis 6:20; 7:14. Observe that it also says in Genesis 1:11 that each fruit has seed within it and, therefore, is self-propagating. The preposition *ek*, from or out of, refers to the direct creative act of God, and *diá*, through, refers to the indirect act of God. Nevertheless, we must not forget that they are all of God. Therefore, "all" means not only all things, but each one in its kind and all kinds put together.

The definite article *toú*, the genitive singular masculine article of *ho*, the, occurs before the word "God." This refers to God the Father (John 1:1). In John 1:3, however, we read, "All *things* through [*diá*] Him [or the Word, referring to the preexistent and co-eternal Christ] were made, and without Him was not anything made that was made." God's design is that every human being comes into the world through a woman, but Jesus Christ is the One through whom all things that exist came to be.

<u>LESSONS</u>:

1. God created all that exists and He put everything in its order.
2. He created man directly, and woman out of the man.
3. He brings forth every human being through a woman, that being His design of procreation.
4. As He permitted a woman to be the instrument through which He brings all humanity into the world, so through Christ, the uncreated Word Himself, He brought about all that there is in creation.

1 Cor. 11:13 | Head Covering Is a Personal Decision

Judge for yourselves. Is it proper for a woman to be uncovered when she prays to God?

In 1 Corinthians chapters 8 through 10, Paul touches upon the nonessentials of Christian conduct. In chapter 11, he discusses the matter of head coverings, continuing his discussion regarding nonessentials. To put it in modern vernacular, as one cannot judge a book by its cover, so one cannot judge another as to the state of his spiritual condition from his external appearance, that is, whether their hair is short or long or their head is covered or uncovered.

However, Paul does give some specific commands which we are to heed. One explicit command Paul gives, which by all means we must obey, is delineated in 1 Corinthians 10:14: "Flee from idolatry." In our personal judgment as to whether we should eat or not eat of meat sacrificed to idols, we should beware lest others think that we in any way approve of idolatry, because that is directly contrary to monotheism. If we go back to 1 Corinthians 6:18, we will encounter another explicit commandment, and that is, "Flee from fornication." We should not give others who observe our behavior the idea that we compromise with sexual sin in any form. The matter of women having short hair or shaven or uncovered heads is related to the sin of fornication. As far as Corinth was concerned, it signified that a woman was available for immoral purposes if she appeared in public with short or shaven hair. Applying this concept to today's culture, we should judge for ourselves if our behavior or dress should in any way intimate promiscuity on our part.

"Judge for Yourselves"

That the issue of head coverings is a personal matter is apparent from this statement: "Judge for yourselves." The verb is *krínate*, the second person plural aorist active imperative of *krínō* (2919), to judge, to decide. The matter of head coverings for women during prayer is not a matter of doctrine essential to salvation, but it is rather a matter of personal judgment. The Corinthians were called upon to make up their own minds and decide what was proper when a Corinthian Christian woman prayed. Paul reminds them of the prevailing circumstances in Corinth. He told them that it was shameful for a man to cover his head and a woman not to cover hers. For a man, the uncovered head signified that he was the head of the woman, especially in marriage. Since a woman in Corinth with short or shaven hair bore the image of being available for prostitution, the Christian woman should avoid such an appearance.

In Greek, this verse begins with the phrase *en* (1722), in; *humín*, the dative plural second person personal pronoun of *sú* (4771), for yourselves; *autoís*, the dative plural masculine personal pronoun of *autós* (846), oneself. This is the only time in the New Testament in which this phrase occurs, and we will do well to examine it closely. It means "in yourselves" or "among yourselves." This is a decision that you yourself must make, without allowing others to influence you. This makes the entire matter of head coverings one of personal choice which cannot be related to those things that constitute the essentials of salvation. This matter was especially critical when a woman was seen praying in the church. If she happened to have short hair or a shaven head when she was saved, she should certainly cover her head when she came into the house of God for prayer, or any other reason.

"Is It Proper for a Woman to Be Uncovered?"

Paul then expresses his opinion which he poses as a question for each individual Christian woman in Corinth to answer for herself: "Is it proper for a woman to be uncovered when she prays to God?"

The Greek word for "Is it proper" is *prépon*, the nominative singular neuter present active participial form of *prépō* (4241), to be becoming, proper, suitable. In the participle, with the verb *eimí* (1510), to be, *estí* is the third person singular present indicative which means, Is it becoming? Is it proper? This phrase is found here and also in Matthew 3:15 in which Jesus said, "It becomes [*prépon*] us to fulfill all righteousness."

In the Christian life, there are some things which we absolutely must believe and which we must do after we are saved. We must believe that God is One in three Persons: God the Father, God the Son, and God the Holy Spirit. We must believe that God is sovereign. We must not have any other gods besides the one true God, nor should we worship graven images. We must not take the name of God in vain. We must not treat the Sabbath day as a common day, but we must distinguish between worship and work. We must have affection for family. We must not kill nor commit adultery. We must not steal, and we must not lie. We must not covet or be greedy. These are the Ten Commandments expressly given in Exodus 20:1–17. They deal with specific circumstances, but there are individual choices that we must make in our daily walk with the Lord. In order to be pleasing to our Lord, we must seek His guidance in matters for which we do not have specific commandments. This is where the conscience comes in. In Paul's instructions to the Corinthian church, he wants them to make proper judgments, considering the significance of a woman's uncovered head in terms of local customs.

"When She Prays to God"

In this verse, Paul speaks only of the Christian woman praying, but he does not include prophesying, as is mentioned in verses 4 and 5. Praying involves having an audience with God, and according to verse 10, praying also means being in the presence of angels who follow us from above. But when prophesying, we are simply in the presence of other human beings to whom we speak. Paul puts emphasis on speaking with God as the most important of all functions of the Christian life. The present infinitive *proseúchesthai*, the present middle deponent infinitive of *proseúchomai* (4336), to pray, indicates continual action of prayer. Paul wanted the Corinthian woman to be conscious of the fact that she is always in the presence of God. By wearing a covering on her head, she demonstrated her submission to God and her desire to be known as a moral person.

LESSONS:

1. We must recognize that in order to be a child of God, we must be born again from above (John 3:3, 7).
2. We must believe that God's Son came into the world to save sinners, such as we are (1 Tim. 1:15; 1 John 4:1–3).
3. We must believe that God is the only One worthy of our worship.
4. Beyond the essentials for which we have specific instructions in the Word of God, there are decisions we must make for ourselves. We should bear in mind local customs and what impressions others, both Christians and non-Christians, may derive from our behavior.

1 Cor. 11:14 | God Established Order in Nature

Or does not even nature itself teach you that, on the one hand, if man grows long hair, it is a dishonor to him?

Paul has pointed out to the Corinthians that a woman should not pray or prophesy with her head uncovered. This was due to local customs indicating that a woman who had short hair or a shaven head was immoral. It is an unnatural appearance. In Romans 1:26, 27, Paul describes lesbianism as a deviation from the natural usage of a woman's body into that which is against nature (*pará* [3844], against; *phúsin*, the accusative singular noun of *phúsis* [5449], nature). In verse 27, Paul speaks of homosexuality as being unnatural. God told us how and why He created man and woman, and how the natural desire of each is for a member of the opposite gender. The word *phúsis*, nature, as it occurs in this verse, refers to the true nature of things as God established them. If we follow its indications, God's design itself becomes a teacher.

"Or Does Not Even Nature Itself Teach You?"

The way that this question is asked necessitates an affirmative, emphatic answer: "Or does not [*ḗ* {2228}, or; *oudé* {3761}, neither, not even, derived from *ou* {3756}, the absolute 'not' and *dé* {1161}, the adversative particle meaning 'but']?"

"Nature itself" comes from *autḗ*, the nominative singular feminine personal pronoun of *autós* (846), himself; *hē*, the nominative singular feminine article of *ho* (3588), the; and *phúsis*, nature. The Greek text says "the nature itself," implying nature as God formed it. Many people today have a perverted nature which is not according to God's original plan (Rom. 1:26). It is true that there are homosexuals and lesbians who are attracted to members of their sex, but this does not coincide with God's original plan for mankind. This behavior is demonstrative of a fallen nature.

"Teach you" is translated from *didáskei*, the third person singular present active indicative of *didáskō* (1321), to teach. Nature, as God designed it, in its original state before the fall, is to be our teacher.

"That, on the One Hand, if a Man Grows Long Hair"

What does nature teach us regarding a man who wears his hair long? The word translated "if" is *eán* (1437), the conjunction of reality, meaning that there actually were some men in Corinth who grew their hair long, just as there are in our day. The verb translated "grows long hair" is *komá*, the third person singular present active subjunctive of *komáō* (2863), to have long hair. This verb is found only in verses 14 and 15 of this chapter. In reference to the verb *komáō*, Liddell and Scott, in their *Greek-English Lexicon* (edition 1882, p. 827), states the following: "for men to wear long hair was considered as a sign of foppery [foolishness, folly] and dissolute habits." So the word *komáō* carries with it the connotation of a careless attitude, the evidence of which in men is long hair.

"It Is a Dishonor to Him"

Paul says that if a man grows his hair long, it is a dishonor to him (*atimía* [819], dishonor, derived from the privative *a* [1] and *timḗ* [5092], honor or attributed value, respect). A man ought to be admired and respected for his strength which is a gift of God. But a man who dishonors himself by wearing long hair shows a lack of appreciation for this gift that God has given him. The woman, on the other hand, complements the man with her softness and her beauty. The outward appearance of both men and women should reflect their acceptance of God's design for their unique identities. For a man to look like a woman is to declare that he considers himself womanly and that he rejects the role God has meant him to play.

The verb that is used to describe the relationship of a woman to a man, especially that of a wife to her husband, is *hupotássomai* (5293), to voluntarily place oneself under (*hupó* [5259]). A wife abides under the care and protection of her husband. In this relationship, a wife's glory comes from her willingness to voluntarily submit to her husband, and the husband's glory comes when he loves his wife as Christ loves the church (Eph. 5:22–29).

LESSONS:

1. God has created man and woman for each other which is the natural order of things.
2. Nature is a teacher from which we can learn.
3. It is not natural for a man to look like a woman, nor a woman to look like a man.
4. Lesbianism and homosexuality are unnatural.
5. God has endowed the man with strength and the woman is to abide under her husband's protection.

1 Cor. 11:15 | *Long Hair or a Covering Is an Honor to a Woman*

But if a woman has long hair, it is a true evaluation of herself, for long hair has been given her in lieu of a head covering.

In this verse we are told what Paul considers to be a natural gift for a woman, that is, her long hair. *Gunḗ* (1135), a woman or female, is contrasted with *anḗr* (435), a man or male of verse 14. The contrast is indicated by the adversative particle *dé* (1161), but.

"But if a Woman Has Long Hair, It Is a True Evaluation of Herself"

The word "if" is the realistic "if" (*eán* [1437]) and not the subjective "if" (*ei* [1487]). There were many women in Corinth who had long hair. If a woman did, it was an indication that she evaluated herself as a moral woman. The phrase is *dóxa* (1391), glory; *autḗ,* to her, the dative singular feminine form of *autós* (846), him; *estín* (2076), is. We have translated "glory" (*dóxa* as "a true evaluation" because it is more accurate since *dóxa* stands in contrast to *atimía* (819), dishonor. If having long hair for a man is a dishonor, an evaluation of himself as being weak, then long hair for a woman is a proper, true evaluation of her femininity.

"For Long Hair Has Been Given in Lieu of a Head Covering.

Paul acknowledges that long hair for a woman is a gift of God. The subject of *dédotai*, the third person singular perfect passive indicative of *dídōmi* (1325), to give, is *komē*, long hair, and God is the source. The long hair of a woman is a natural covering, whereas the *peribólaion* (4018), a covering around the head, is an artificial covering. If for any reason a woman lacked naturally long hair, it would be becoming for her to cover her head with a hat or a scarf since the figurative significance of it indicated a moral character.

LESSONS:

1. Long hair, which is a dishonor for a man, is an honor for a woman.
2. Long hair for a woman is a gift of God.
3. In the absence of long hair, a woman was encouraged to wear a head covering in demonstration of her moral character.

1 Cor. 11:16 | *Let Us Not Be Quarrelsome*

If anyone seems to be quarrelsome, we have no such custom, nor do the churches of God.

There are many things which can divide the church of God, and throughout the book of 1 Corinthians, Paul has been dealing with some of them. As the parts of the human body are different, so is the body of Christ, each member complementing the others. There is beauty in individuality, but a believer who is controlled by the love of Christ is not devisive. Paul advises the believers to be respectful of the customs of others and to let each one decide for himself or herself on nonessential matters.

"If Anyone Seems to Be Quarrelsome"

The verse begins with the subjective "if" or *ei* (1487). It is different than the realistic "if" or *eán* (1437) which has been used in previous verses. Paul is giving us the idea that we show our true character by the subjects on which we choose to elaborate or create factions.

We have translated *tis* (5100) as "anyone," because it is the singular masculine indefinite pronoun: "If anyone seems [*dokeí*, the third person singular present active indicative form of *dokéō* {1380}, to think, to seem] to be quarrelsome [*philóneikos* {5380}, quarrelsome, derived from *phílos* [5384], a friend, and *neíkos*, which is not found in the NT but means a quarrel, dispute, strife]." Unfortunately, there are too many Christians who assume a contentious attitude over certain practices or customs. This is the only verse in the New Testament in which the word *philóneikos* occurs. Evidently, the Corinthian church had plenty of contentious people!

"We Have No Such Custom"

Paul, however, stresses that such was not his philosophy of life. He includes in this category other Christians, and this is why he said, "We [*hēmeis* {2249}] do not have such a custom" [*sunḗtheian*, the accusative singular feminine noun of *sunḗtheia* {4914}, custom; *ouk*, the absolute *ou* {3756}, not, which takes the *k* at the end since the following verb begins with a vowel; *échomen*, the first person plural present active indicative of *échō* {2192}, to have].

When Paul says, "**we** do not have such a custom," undoubtedly he included the other apostles and leaders of local churches. In 1 Corinthians 4:9, he uses the word "we" in the same manner to distinguish between the worldly progress some believers had been able to accomplish in contrast to what the destiny of the apostles had been. Whereas the believers had advanced in the things of the world and become successful and proud, "we," the Apostle says, have proven to be the last and are ready to die at any time. "We have been made a spectacle to the world, to angels, and to men."

The word for "custom" is *sunḗtheia*, which is derived from the preposition *sún* (4862), denoting joint togetherness; and *ḗthos* (2239), a moral custom pertaining to character (1 Cor. 15:33). It is from this word that our English word "ethics" is derived. We see, therefore, that throughout history an imposed custom or one that had developed naturally may become part of accepted morality. The word *éthos* (1485) occurs in reference to a custom of the priests in Luke 1:9; the custom of the feast

(Luke 2:42); the usual thing to do (Luke 22:39); or the usual thing to do by a certain group of people such as the Jews (John 19:40), and as the customs that came down from a leader such as Moses (Acts 6:14; 15:1). In Acts 21:21, Paul is accused of saying that the Jews among the Gentiles did not have to follow the Jewish customs. In his defense before King Agrippa in Acts 26:3, Paul appeals to Agrippa's knowledge of the Jewish customs. In his argument, Paul stresses his own Jewish background (vv. 4, 5). In Acts 28:17, he claims that in his behavior he did nothing against the customs of the fathers thereby offending the Jews. (See also Acts 16:21; 25:16; Heb. 10:25.)

The word *sunḗtheia*, custom, can have the meaning of an individual accepting an idea without questioning it, and when it becomes a habit, it is followed without consideration. On the other hand, a custom (*éthos*) may be something that is accepted by a community because it is done by most individuals.

Apparently, the Apostles practiced certain customs, one of which was the avoidance of discussions that would lead to contention. It was a principle that the Apostles developed, although, being only human, they did not always succeed in that area. Paul had a disagreement with Peter (Gal. 2:11–21) which was based on a doctrinal matter. The Apostles did not argue among themselves, however, over unimportant customs that pervaded the Christian church. Therefore, the denial of the custom of head coverings has the absolute negative *ouk* on the part of Paul and the other Apostles in his comment, "Such a custom we do not have [*ouk échomen*]."

The word *ḗthos* occurs only once in 1 Corinthians in 15:33 where it should be translated "moral habits." The Apostles did not pursue discussions that would lead to divisions among Christians, especially if those discussions were on matters that were not essential (*adiáphora*) to salvation.

In addition to verse 16 under study, the word *sunḗtheia*, custom, is used in John 18:39 where Pilate said to the Jews who wanted to crucify Christ, "But you have a custom [*sunḗtheia*] that I should release unto you one at Passover: Will you therefore that I release unto you the king of the Jews?" It is also in the Critical Text of 1 Corinthians 8:10, which the Textus Receptus and the Majority Text have as *suneídēsis* (4983), conscience, and which we preferred as stated in the examination of that verse. It shows, however, that there were certain customs which were accepted by the general public but were rejected by the Apostles, because those customs led to undesirable results. The principle set forth by the Apostle Paul is that there can be conformity to customs if that conformity is not contrary to the basics of the gospel. In the case of women having their heads covered, it was a custom in Corinth for which adequate support in the Scriptures can be found. Paul finds the opportunity, in discussing this custom, also to support the idea of short hair for men. At the end of the discussion, however, he states that his motive was not to be contentious, as this was totally against the apostolic principles.

"Nor Do the Churches of God"

Paul closes this discussion by stating, "nor do the churches of God." This is *oudḗ* (3761), neither, nor, derived from the absolute negative *ou*, not, and *dé* (1161), but.

This is the only Scripture in which we find the expression "the churches of God [*haí* {3588}, the plural feminine article 'the'; *ekklēsíai*, the nominative plural feminine form of the noun *hē ekklēsía* {1577}, the church; *toú* {5120}, of the, the genitive singular masculine article of *ho*, the; *Theoú*, God, the genitive singular masculine noun of *Theós* {2316}, God]." The first time that the word "church" appears in the New Testament is in Matthew 16:18 when the Lord said to Peter that on his confession that He was the Christ, the Son of the Living God, He would build His church. In Romans 16:16, Paul calls the local churches the "churches of Christ." This is another affirmation that Christ is God. The churches of Christ are the churches of God. It is used in the plural here to demonstrate that the church of Christ or of God is made up of local churches which are not usually identified in the Scriptures by their particular doctrines, as happens today, but by the location in which they were found (Acts 8:1; 11:22; Rom. 16:1; 1 Cor. 16:1, 19; 2 Cor. 1:1; 8:1; Gal. 1:2; Col. 4:16; 1 Thess. 1:1; Rev. 2:1, 8, 12, 18; 3:1, 7, 14). In studying the Scriptures, we can discern that the different churches had different customs, but these customs were not to become divisive issues. Today, unfortunately, churches are known by their particular doctrines which they stress as being important. Rather than stress their unity in Christ, they emphasize the differences they have with other Christians which indicates that they are *philóneikoi*, lovers of strife or that which differs. We have allowed the local church to succumb to the divisiveness to which Paul declared himself to be in opposition, and he included in that declaration all the local churches at the time. What a wonderful testimony it would be if we could repeat in our day the testimony of the Apostle Paul, that the churches of God or the churches of Christ do not love such divisiveness and contention. To allow such things as head coverings of women to divide the churches is tragic.

LESSONS:

1. Every local church, with its self-government, ought to follow the apostolic teaching and the teaching that is common to all the churches of God or of Christ.
2. A precautionary measure against divisiveness is to not spend precious time in discussions about things that do not make a basic difference.

3. The customs and practices of the local church should not be imposed as doctrine, but the unity of the Spirit of God should lead each local group to decide for itself what to believe.
4. Each local church should view imposed doctrine and practices with apprehension.

1 Cor. 11:17 | *Paul's Personal Recommendation*

But as I am personally recommending—I do not praise you at all—that you gather together with others for the better, not for the worse.

In our examination of verse 2, we saw that the verb *katéchete* (2722), to hold fast or faithfully as was given, should be taken as an imperative and not as an active indicative. Paul was telling the Corinthians to keep the traditions (*paradóseis* [3862]) as he had delivered them. This should be their concern in their remembrance of him. The truth of the matter, however, is that Paul had personally delivered to the Corinthians certain instructions which they were not keeping. In the noun *paradóseis a*, traditions, and the verb *parédōka*, I delivered, the prefix is *pará* (3844), a preposition that indicates intimacy. The same is true of the verb *paralambánō* (3880), to receive from, which occurs in 1 Corinthians 11:23. Paul's two epistles to the Corinthians do not contain much for which to praise them, but much which they needed to correct.

"But *as* I Am Personally Recommending"

The participle "personally recommending" that Paul is using in this verse also has the prepositional prefix *pará*. It is *paraggéllōn*, the nominative singular masculine present active participial form of *paraggéllō* (3853), from *pará*, being beside you, and *aggéllō*, to declare. *Aggéllō* is not found as a basic verb in the New Testament, although it is found as *anaggéllō* (312), to tell, declare. *Paraggéllō* implies that a request is made in closeness and intimacy. The verb *paraggéllō* was also used in 1 Corinthians 7:10 by the Apostle Paul, himself evidently a bachelor, and would be better translated, "And unto the married I personally [or intimately] recommend, yet not I, but the Lord, let not the wife depart from her husband."

The fact that the verb is in the present participial form indicates that what Paul had already suggested, as well as what he continues to say, is his own advice. This is especially so in these chapters in which he is dealing with matters that are essential to one's salvation and for which there is no biblical standard by which one could make an absolute rule. The people who received these recommendations from him should consider them as such—the recommendations of an Apostle (1 Cor. 9:1) to the local churches of God. Thus to give understanding of the present participle, we have included the adverb "as."

"I Do Not Praise You at All"

Paul, however, did not want these recommendations to be considered as praise for the Corinthian believers, for they needed much cultivation of their Christian character. For this reason Paul brought up these nonessential matters. He expressed this caution with the absolute "not" (*ouk* [3756] with an added *k* because the next word, *epainṓ*, begins with a vowel). Twice (see also 1 Cor. 11:22) Paul emphatically states that he is not praising the Corinthians for their behavior. The only time Paul uses *epainṓ* in a positive way is in verse 2 which, however, is restrictive in its meaning (see the exegesis of this verse). In verse 2 Paul is praising the Corinthians that they remembered what he taught them. He pleads with them, however, to remember his teaching exactly as he had given it and to hold to it. *Epainṓ* is the contracted form of *epainéō* (1867) which is derived from *epí* (1909), "upon" which indicates concentration, and *ainéō* (134), to praise. Paul's personal correction, should not be mistaken as praise. He did not want his praise of verse 2 to be misunderstood. Nor did he want the unbiblical social customs which had permeated their religious practices to influence them in any way as Christians.

"That You Gather Together With Others for the Better, Not for the Worse"

The verb "you gather together with others" is *sunérchesthe*, the second person plural present middle deponent indicative of *sunérchomai* (4905), to gather together. In the next verse, Paul admonishes the Corinthians that when they gather for church services, it should be for the better (*kreítton* or *kreísson* [2908]) and not for the worse. How wonderful it would be if every time we attended church, it resulted in our being better Christians, ". . . and not for the worse" [*hḗtton* or *hḗsson* {2276}, used as an irregular comparative of *kakós* {2556}, bad, evil]. We would do well, after each service, to examine ourselves and to see if our behavior has had a positive rather than a negative effect on those with whom we have come in contact.

This verse stands in the middle of Paul's discussions regarding the impressions that we make on others from what we eat and drink to the way we wear our hair. We are to do all things for the glory of God and the edification of the saints.

LESSONS:

1. Paul could not greatly praise the Corinthians, but he tried to make personal recommendations for their private and church gatherings.
2. It was Paul's desire that every church gathering make us spiritually better and not worse.

1 Cor. 11:18 | Divisions in the Church

For first of all, when you gather together as a church, I hear that there exist among you divisions, and I believe part of it.

In the eleventh chapter of 1 Corinthians Paul has dealt in detail with the behavior of the members of the Corinthian church, and he is concerned lest their gathering be for the worse, and not the better. In this verse, he continues to address the problem.

"For First of All"

This phrase is translated from *prṓton* (4412), the neuter form of *prṓtos* (4413), first, and is used as an adverb to emphasize that for which the church in Corinth was known; *mén* (3303), a conjunction implying affirmation but pointing back to something which is opposite and is usually expressed by *dé* (1161), "but" used strictly as an adversative in Matthew 3:11; 9:37, etc. This adversative is also found in verse 28 in which Paul says, "**But** let each man examine himself, and so let him eat of that bread, and drink of that cup." Paul speaks of the reputation of the Corinthian church as he has heard from others, and his appeal is that each man should examine his behavior in the church. He considered the behavior of believers as the most important thing, for it is of great concern that the church should be preserved in the unity of the Spirit (Eph. 4:3, 13).

"When You Gather Together"

Again, as in 1 Corinthians 11:17, we find the word *sunerchoménōn*, the genitive plural masculine present middle deponent participle of *sunérchomai* (4905), to gather or to come together. The Apostle Paul uses the present tense to indicate that this is a customary and necessary gathering together for a common purpose. The Corinthian believers meet together to affirm and declare the work of grace upon their lives and to recognize that they are all members of one body, the body of Christ (1 Cor. 12:13).

Another occurrence of *sunérchomai*, gather together, is found in verse 20 in which Paul advises the Corinthians that their church gatherings should not be characterized by eating and drinking. It is also found in verses 33 and 34 in which Paul states that their gathering together should not be for the purpose of finding fault with one another. This word is also found in 1 Corinthians 14:23 in which their gathering together was described as giving the appearance of a madhouse since all spoke at once. Again in verse 26, Paul advises that a church service in all its various parts should be conducted orderly for edification.

"As a Church"

The expression "as a church" is *en* (1722), in; *ekklēsía,* the dative singular feminine noun of *ekklēsía* (1577), church, assembly. Paul reminds the Corinthians that they should be conscious of the purpose for which they congregate. In their gathering together for church, they constitute a group of people who have "come out," as the meaning of *ekklēsía* conveys. It is from the preposition *ek* (1537), out of, and the verb *kaléō* (2564), to call. A church consists of those who are called out of the sinful world to constitute a separate group of people. When believers live with the constant consciousness of being distinctly different because of the miracle of the new birth (John 3:3, 7), they find strength and encouragement in fellowship with those of like precious faith.

This is one of four places in the Corinthian epistles that Paul uses the expression, *en ekklēsía*, and it means in a local assembly or church service. In this verse, Paul implies that when believers gather together, they should not allow unimportant issues to divide them into factions.

The second time we find the expression "in church" is in 1 Corinthians 14:19, "Yet in *the* church I had rather speak five words with my understanding [*toú noós*, the genitive singular masculine noun of *noús* {3563}, mind] that by my voice I might teach others also, than ten thousand words in an *unknown* tongue." Paul states that when believers gather together in church, it is not a time to disengage their minds, but to use them in order to instruct others or learn for themselves. The only way to learn is to understand.

The third time that the expression "in *the* church" occurs is in 1 Corinthians 14:28 in which Paul says, "But if there be no interpreter, let him keep silence in *the* church; and let him speak to himself, and to God." To speak in church in a language that others do not understand is prohibited.

And the fourth time that "in church" occurs is in 1 Corinthians 14:35 in speaking of wives. Here Paul says, "And if they will learn anything, let them ask their husbands at home for it is a shame for women [wives] to speak in church." Wives were not to question their husbands in church about what was being said, but were to wait until they got home. Evidence indicates that the women sat upstairs in the balcony while the men sat downstairs. Since there was no sound system as we use today, the women often could not hear all that was being said and called to their husbands who were sitting below to ask for clarification.

"I Hear That There Exist Among You Divisions"

"I hear" is translated from *akoúō* (191), the first person present active indicative. Paul did not have his ears closed as to what was going on in the Corinthian church.

The verb which we chose to translate "exist" is *hupárchein*, the present active infinitive of *hupárchō* (5225) which is derived from *hupó* (5259), under, and *árchō* (757), to. It is interesting, indeed, that the Apostle does not use the verb *eisín* (1526), there are, which would indicate that the divisions exist only in the present. The use of the verb *hupárchō* indicates that the past had something to do with it, that these divisions were preexistent, and that they were not entirely to be blamed on persons such as Apollos, Cephas, Christ, or Paul as mentioned in 1 Corinthians 1:12, 13. They were due to the predispositions of the Corinthians. To illustrate the meaning of *hupárchō*, one should turn to Philippians 2:6 where Paul says, "Who [Christ] in the form of God existing [*hupárchōn*] from the beginning." Christ always was God, even prior to His incarnation, and He continues to be.

We translated the word "divisions" from *schísmata*, the accusative plural neuter noun of *schísma* (4978), split, schism, division, which comes from *schízō* (4977), to split or tear apart. A schism is a division, a faction. In John 7:43; 9:16; 10:19, we find that Jesus' teachings and miracles caused divisions among many. The same was true with the life and words of Paul. The word *schísmata*, divisions, occurs for the first time in Paul's Epistles in 1 Corinthians 1:10. These schisms or splits were associated with the contentions (*érides*, the nominative plural feminine noun of *éris* [2054], strife, contention, wrangling) among the Corinthians. (See also Rom. 13:13; 1 Cor. 1:11;

3:3; 2 Cor. 12:20; Gal. 5:20; Phil. 1:15; 1 Tim. 6:4; Titus 3:9.) Divisions in Corinth revolved around following individual leaders such as Paul, Apollos, and Cephas (Peter). The most appalling thing that these divisions did among the Corinthians was to equate these human leaders with Christ. This is why Paul asks, Who was crucified for you? (1 Cor. 1:10–17). Elevating an individual leader to a place of worship always leads to strife and contention. No other church is characterized as having as many divisions as the Corinthian church.

The Apostle Paul did not want to see confusion and divisions in the local church. The phrase *en ekklēsía*, in church, in this verse, tells us that it is undesirable in a local congregation to have schisms, parties, and divisions. This brings to mind 1 Corinthians 1:10–13 where Paul told the Corinthians that it was known that there were factions among them:

> Now, I beseech you, brethren, by the name of our Lord Jesus Christ, that you all speak the same thing, and that there be no divisions [*schísmata*, schisms] among you; but that you be perfectly joined together in the same mind and in the same judgment. For it has been declared unto me of you, my brethren, by them which are of the house of Chloe, that there are contentions among you. Now this I say, that every one of you says, I am of Paul; and I of Apollos; and I of Cephas; and I of Christ. Is Christ divided? Was Paul crucified for you? Or were you baptized in the name of Paul?

"And I Believe Part of It"

Paul was cautious about the reports he heard regarding the Corinthian church, and he examined them to see just how much was believable. Upon his investigation, he found part of them false and part true. It was his desire to correct the Corinthians, since the information came from reliable sources, such as the household of Chloe. Although he did not take every word he heard as the truth, he was not afraid to deal with the parts that were true, for that was the only way to correct the problem.

In 1 Corinthians 5:1, Paul wrote, "It is reported commonly that there is fornication among you, and such fornication as is not so much as named among the Gentiles, that one should have his father's wife." He did not hesitate to name the sin of this immoral young man. We find as we read further that Paul was able to help the Corinthian believers deal with this problem and that, in the end, the young man repented.

> Sufficient to such a man is this punishment, which was inflicted of many. So that contrariwise you ought rather to forgive him, and comfort him, lest perhaps such a one should be swallowed up with overmuch sorrow. Wherefore I beseech you that you would confirm your love toward him (2 Cor. 2:6–8).

It seems that there was sin not only on the part of the immoral young man in this case, but also on the part of many in the congregation due to their harsh and unforgiving attitude, for Paul speaks of the "punishment inflicted by many." He urges the Corinthian Christians to forgive this man and to let him know that they love him. Evidently their punishment had been severe, and Paul is gently telling them, Enough is enough! How easy it is for us as Christians in our detestation of sin to detest the sinner also. We learn through Paul's advice to the Corinthian Christians that this should not be.

Paul did not have an ear for criticism of the churches only, but for commendation as well. In Ephesians 1:15, 16a, he wrote, "Wherefore I also after I heard of your faith in the Lord Jesus, and love unto all the saints, cease not to give thanks for you." Whereas in Corinth, he heard of divisions, in Philippi it was otherwise, for he commends them saying, "Only let your conversation be as it becomes the gospel of Christ: that whether I come and see you, or else be absent, I may hear of your affairs, that you stand fast in one spirit, with one mind striving together for the faith of the gospel" (Phil. 1:27). In the same spirit of commendation, he writes in Colossians 1:4, "Since we heard of your faith in Christ Jesus, and of the love which you have to all the saints." In verse 5, he says to Philemon, "Hearing of your love and faith, which you have toward the Lord Jesus, and toward all saints." Correction is necessary at times, but love and encouragement are needed even more.

LESSONS:

1. We bear a responsibility as Christians, when we gather together with others, to preserve the unity of the Spirit.
2. When we gather for church and in church, we should endeavor to accomplish the purposes for which the church exists, the worship of God and the building up of the saints.
3. We should have nothing to do with gatherings if they are factional and if there is a following of individual leaders.
4. We should examine the truth about what we hear and not encourage divisions.
5. We should not render a deaf ear to complaints or praises of a certain group, but neither should we believe all the gossip we hear.

1 Cor. 11:19 | Heresies Can Serve a Purpose

Nevertheless, heresies are unavoidable among you for the purpose of manifesting who among you are able to become approved.

We read in 1 Corinthians 1:10 Paul's appeal to the Corinthian believers to avoid divisions or schisms. Nevertheless, we find later in the book (11:18) that, in fact, divisions did exist. Paul tries to encourage these Christians to be of the same mind and not to follow individual leaders. In the verse we will study now, however, Paul says that heresies, which are the seeds that can grow into schisms, are unavoidable.

"Nevertheless, Heresies Are Unavoidable Among You"

The first thing that we ought to examine is the meaning of the word "heresies" which is a transliteration of the word *hairéseis*, the accusative plural feminine noun of *haíresis* (139). Two words, *schísmata*, divisions (v. 18), and *hairéseis* (v. 19), are used in this passage. The verb from which *schísma* is derived is *schízō* (4977), to split, sever, divide. *Schísma* involves not only individual choice of thought, but also attachment to a specific leader.

We have translated the word *deí* (1163), must, the third person singular present indicative impersonal form of *déō* (1210), needs be, as "unavoidable" or inevitable in the nature of things.

Deí is an abbreviation of *déon esti,* it is necessary. In the realm of thought, it expresses necessity of logic or science. It can also denote ethical or necessary compliance to design, as, for instance, a person must eat because God has designed that human beings take nourishment from food. God also designed man to exercise a free will which entails responsibility for his actions. Consequences of each decision are unavoidable, which is the meaning of the word *deí.*

We have translated *gár* (1063) as "nevertheless," because a contrast is drawn here between the two words *schísmata,* schisms, which should be avoided in the Christian church, and *hairéseis,* heresies. The noun *haíresis,* heresy, comes from the verb *hairéō* (138), to choose, select. In the New Testament, heresy is a departure from truth (see Acts 5:17; 15:5; 24:5, 14; 26:5; 28:22; 1 Cor. 11:19; Gal. 5:20; 2 Pet. 2:1). In contrast to *schísma,* schism, which is an actual tearing apart, heresy may represent a divergent opinion but still be part of the whole. One can hold a different view than the majority and still remain in the same body, although he is a heretic (*hairetikós,* [141]). However, when he tears himself completely away (*schízō*), then he is schismatic. Heresy may lead to schism, which is the actual tearing apart and separation.

Paul declares in this verse that heresies are unavoidable, because, upon becoming a Christian, an individual does not cease to exercise freedom of thought and decision since God has thus designed the human mind. Twice in 1 Corinthians the Apostle Paul says, "All things are permissible to me" (6:12; 10:23), for a radical change had occurred and he became a slave of Jesus Christ (Rom. 6:18, 19). Paul understood that he was a free man (Rom. 6:20), not free to serve sin and Satan, but free to voluntarily obey Christ and to choose ways to express that freedom. The chains of sin had been broken (1 Cor. 9:19). In the case of Paul, his motive and purpose was to win as many souls to Christ as possible. In order to do that, he chose that which was mutually beneficial to all believers (*sumphéron* [4851]; see 1 Cor. 6:12; 10:23). Paul believed that choices regarding things that were nonessential (*adiáphora*) should be decided upon by each individual Christian once his loyalty was transferred from Satan to Christ. However, when it came to the basic issue of the new birth, the word that is used is *deí*, must. This is the word Christ used when he said to Nicodemus, "You must (*deí*) be born again" (John 3:7). This applies to all unregenerate people. But all too often, we have allowed the freedom that we have in Christ to become a hindrance to our full dedication to the Lord rather than the blessing which Christ Himself ordained. This is why, in the middle of a detailed discussion concerning the nonessentials of the Christian life, Paul, in 1 Corinthians 9:24–27, presents the Christian life as a race for which there is a reward at the end.

"For the Purpose of Manifesting"

Paul reveals the purpose of our freedom of action as children of God. This is why we chose to translate *hína* (2443), in order that, as "for the purpose of." Although we have been born into the family of God, we still have the privilege of individual choice. The choices that we voluntarily make as believers show whether or not we are really genuine Christians. The ones being tested (*dókima* [1384]) will be made (*génōntai*, third person plural second aorist middle deponent subjunctive of *gínomai* [1096]) manifest (*phaneroí*, the nominative plural middle form of the adjective *phanerós* [5318], apparent).

"Who Among You Are Able to Become Approved"

The phrase "are able to become" is a translation of the verb *génōntai*, the third person plural second aorist middle deponent subjunctive of the verb *gínomai*, to become. The usage of the aorist subjunctive shows that there is a specific point in time at which one becomes acceptable to the Lord and is placed in His body. Becoming approved and acceptable to the Lord is known to Him immediately when it occurs, but it is made evident to others as the new believer begins to study the Word of God and obey His Lord. This change becomes obvious through the transformation of character and the consequent individual choices which preserve the unity of the Spirit within the local church.

The word *dókimoi* (1384), approved, is the opposite of the word *adókimos* (96), unapproved, as found in 1 Corinthians 9:27. *Dókimoi* means proved and accepted to run the Christian race, whereas *adókimos* means having been rejected as not having had the miraculous change that one must experience, the necessary change resulting from the new birth into the family of God. Evidently there were many people in the church of Corinth who thought they were born again, but their behavior demonstrated that they were anything but. The same is true in the Christian church today. Nonbelievers gather together with true believers, but in reality they are not one with them because they have not been born again, and so it is impossible for them to be diligent in preserving the unity of the spirit (Eph. 4:3).

There is the definite article "the" in the plural before the word *dókimoi*, meaning that there was a certain point in time when a person became born again and passed the test of having been truly regenerated from above (John 3:3, 7). Whether he has been born from above or not becomes evident from his actions in the church and the things he chooses to do or not to do. A person cannot be only partly born again.

The point at which the manifestation of the new birth and the nature of God within one's heart becomes evident (2 Pet. 1:4) is expressed by the word *phaneroí*, the plural of *phanerós*. It usually takes time to evidence the new birth among fellow believers. However, to our omniscient God, this is known from the moment of repentance and belief.

All choices of a Christian ought to promote the gospel. Although true Christians all have the mind of Christ (1 Cor. 2:16), Paul recognizes that as individuals they exercise freedom of thought and choice but differ in their degree of dedication to the Lord. If they do not have the mind of Christ and if they act independently of Him, then they are not of Christ.

LESSONS:

1. God gave man the ability to choose to confess his sin and to ask for forgiveness. This is absolutely necessary for salvation.
2. God knows the moment a man's saving faith is exercised.
3. It takes time for faith to be made manifest to fellow believers.
4. A man is a true believer when he manifests the mind of Christ and when his individual choices align with the Lord's revealed will.

1 Cor. 11:20 | *Meeting Together Is Not for Eating*

As you meet together in the same location, it is not for eating Sunday supper.

In verse 18, Paul chided the Corinthians because their meetings together did not demonstrate the unity of the Spirit, for there were divisions within their local body.

"As You Meet Together in the Same Location"

This verse begins with the verb *sunerchoménōn* as does verse 18. It is the genitive plural masculine present middle deponent participial form of *sunérchomai* (4905), to come together, and it indicates any gathering together.

It is important to realize that as the believers gathered together in one place (*epí* [1909], upon; *tó*, the accusative singular neuter article of *ho* [3588], the; *autṓ*, the dative singular neuter personal pronoun of *autós* [846], same, implying place or location), it was primarily a social event for them.

"It Is Not for Eating Sunday Supper"

Let us first examine the noun translated "supper," which is *deípnon* (1173), the chief meal which was eaten usually in the evening (Luke 14:12, 16, 17, 24; John 12:2; 13:2, 4; 21:20; 1 Cor. 11:20, 21; Rev. 19:9, 17; cf. Mark 6:21). Of the two daily meals common to the Jews in New Testament times, supper was the most important. It was usually eaten about sunset or shortly thereafter (Luke 14:12; 17:7, 8). The other meal was called *áriston* (712), dinner, and it was a lighter meal, being eaten about noon or a little before. Prayer was offered before eating either meal (Matt. 14:19; 15:36; Luke 9:16; 22:17; John 6:11; Acts 27:35). In the Corinthian epistles, *deípnon*, supper, is found only here in 1 Corinthians 11:20, 21. There is no doubt that reference is made to an evening meal.

What is translated as "Sunday" is the adjective *kuriakón*, the accusative singular neuter adjective of *kuriakós* (2960), of the Lord. Strictly speaking, the translation of this word means "pertaining to the first day of the week," which has come to be known as *kuriakḗ*, the day belonging to the Lord, or the day of which He is the owner (Rev. 1:10). This was the day of the Lord's resurrection (1 Cor. 15:3, 4). As R. C. H. Lenski says, "The Jews had no names for the weekdays and, therefore, designated them with reference to the Sabbath. Thus, 'on the first day' with reference to the Sabbath, 'that is to say, the first that follows the Sabbath' " (Matt. 28:1; Mark 16:2, 9; Luke 24:1; John 20:1, 19; Acts 20:7; 1 Cor. 16:2). Regarding John 20:1, he further says, "The plural *sábbata* [4521], sabbaths, however, may mean either the Sabbath day, designated with a plural like the festivals in order to include all that belongs to the festival celebration; or an entire week, a length of time bounded by two Sabbaths. Thus, we may here translate, 'on the first day of the week.' Since John wrote for Greek readers, the latter translation seems preferable." (*John's Gospel*, p. 1333)

The question we must consider is whether Paul refers here to the Communion service (or the Lord's Supper, as it has come to be known) or whether it represents common meals eaten at church on Sundays (Acts 20:7) or possibly on undesignated days (Acts 2:46). The Corinthians were gathering together in one place, and we learned in verse 18 that this place was "the church." It was in the church that they were to partake of the cup of blessing which was a reminder of the fellowship and the blood of Christ (1 Cor. 10:16, 21) and were to partake of the bread which was to remind them of their participation in the body of Christ (1 Cor. 10:16, 17). The church was to be a place in which they gathered together to worship and remember their Lord, and not just a place to eat. This was especially so on Sundays when they gathered together in commemoration of the resurrection of the Lord Jesus. In Jude 12, we find that local Christian churches had "love feasts" (*agápais*, the plural of *agápē* [26], love feast, charity celebration) in order to show that the church was a place where love was not only preached, but practiced by helping the poor. However, in these love feasts there were some who were *spiládes*, hidden reefs, who caused others to make shipwrecks of their faith. This is the only place that the word *spilás* (4694) is used in reference to false teachers. This word is variously translated as "spots" (KJV) and "blemishes" (RSV, NIV). The King James Version describes these "spots" in the latter part of Jude 12: "Feeding themselves without fear: clouds they are without water, carried about of winds; trees whose fruit wither, without fruit, twice dead, plucked up by the roots." In 2 Peter 2:13, we read of the same people: "And [they] shall receive the reward of unrighteousness, as they count it pleasure to riot in the daytime. Spots [*spíloi*, the plural of *spílos* {4696}, a spot, a stain, figuratively in a moral sense] they are and blemishes, sporting themselves with their own deceivings while they feast with you." The date which 1 Corinthians was written was approximately A.D. 57, when the love feasts were occurring. The love feasts had degenerated from their original purpose, however, to include undesirable practices and even drunkenness (1 Cor. 11:21) by the time 2 Peter and Jude were written between A.D. 65 and A.D. 68.

However, the love feasts were closely associated to the memorial service of the crucifixion of the Lord Jesus which was a serious and holy commemoration that the Apostle Paul discusses in 1 Corinthians 11:33, 34. There is full justification, therefore, in translating *kuriakón deípnon* as "Sunday supper" and not as the "Lord's Supper." Sunday supper was a meal eaten at the church that should have been eaten at home, Paul explains.

To the early church, eating supper at church was mixed up with the Lord's Supper. Christ had instituted the Lord's Supper in Matthew 26:26–30, Mark 14:22–26, and Luke 22:14–20 after He ate with His disciples on the night before He was crucified. Observe the word *esthíō* (2068), to eat, in various forms in Matthew 26:26, and the verb *phágō* (5315), to eat, in Mark 14:12, 14 and Luke 22:15, 16, and the expression "after supper" of Luke 22:20.

LESSONS:

1. The gathering together in church by Christians is not primarily for purposes of eating and fellowship.
2. The "love feast" as it originated in Corinth became a degenerative practice as we can deduce from Jude 12 and 2 Peter 2:13.
3. It is impossible that Paul condemned the Lord's Supper as we know it today. He condemned Sunday suppers in church, for although they started with a benevolent purpose, they degenerated to occasions of reveling, rioting, and even drunkenness.

1 Cor. 11:21 | *The Responsibility of Eating in the Church*

As each one, therefore, hurries to take his own supper, on the one hand, someone goes hungry; and on the other hand, someone gets drunk.

Paul was concerned about the behavior of those who used the church as a place for eating common meals (v. 18), which he calls Sunday suppers. He wanted those who participated to be conscious of others who were there also and to consider what they would think of the place and the participants. Would they think that the church is a place where personal privilege is maintained and displayed? Would they come to the conclusion that the "love feasts" were actual "spots" and "blemishes" on the Christian church (2 Pet. 2:13; Jude 12)?

Paul previously examined the responsibility of a Christian believer insofar as eating meats sacrificed to idols was concerned. This referred to what he ate either privately in his own home or in a home to which he had been invited (1 Cor. 10:24–33). He also encouraged the Corinthian believers not to participate in the actual feasts at the idol temples, for that would be fellowship with devils (1 Cor. 10:20).

Paul now handles the question of believers and unbelievers who gather to eat and celebrate the feast of love in the church (1 Cor. 11:18). He knows that what an individual is in his own heart and home, he will also be in public. First Corinthians 11 is a defense of the public image of the church as demonstrated by the private character of individuals. What would be the public image of eating a common meal called Sunday supper in the church? Sunday was indeed observed as the day when Christians came together to celebrate the resurrection of Jesus Christ. This was the first day of the week (Acts 20:7; Rev. 1:10) and was called the Lord's Day (*Kuríou*, of the Lord).

"As Each One, Therefore"

In this verse, Paul expresses the responsibility of each individual, believer and unbeliever, in regard to their behavior when assembling and having common meals together in the church. Thus he begins this verse with *hékastos* (1538), the nominative singular masculine adjective meaning each one as an individual. He is concerned about the public image of the church reflected by the behavior of the individuals participating in the love feasts. This refers to each one, whether believer or unbeliever. Since true believers cannot be drunkards, Paul must include nonbelievers in this verse. It was common for nonbelievers to mix with believers, because they enjoyed the public meals. But at these public meals, their unregenerate nature was evident. Paul was concerned that they should keep their drunken behavior in their own private homes and not export it to the local church. In Ephesians 5:18, Paul writes, "And be not drunk with wine, wherein is excess; but be filled with the Spirit."

"Hurries to Take His Own Supper"

What we translated as "hurries to take" is *prolambánei*, the third person singular present active indicative of *prolambánō* (4301), derived from *pró* (4253), before, and *lambánō* (2983), to take. The compound verb means to overtake, to hurry. We have rendered this phrase as "hurries to take his own supper," since the purpose was to eat (*phageín*, the second aorist active infinitive of *esthíō* [2068], to eat) quickly before others had an opportunity to take the food. And what was the outcome of such greediness? Those who did not have anything to eat at home and who came to the Sunday supper at church did not get anything to eat there either. This feast called the "love feast" brought the "have-nots" to church where those who had food were supposed to express love by bringing enough for others as well as themselves. It was evident that it was known as a "love feast" only in name, not in practice.

"His own" is translated from *tó*, the accusative singular neuter article of *ho* (3588), the; *ídion*, the accusative singular neuter adjective of *ídios* (2398), one's own or pertaining to a private person. This person considered what he possessed to be his very own, whether at home or in public. At these "love feasts" those who had food to eat at home would bring it to church, but it seems that they brought only enough for themselves and not for others. It was their own supper to be consumed in public by them alone or perhaps with their special friends.

"On the One Hand, Someone Goes Hungry; and on the Other Hand, Someone Gets Drunk"

Paul adds, "On the one hand [*mén* {3303}, as the first part of a contrast to be drawn], someone goes hungry [*peiná*, the third person singular present active subjunctive of *peináō* {3983}, to go hungry]; and on the other hand [*dé* {1161}, but, the second part of the contrast; *mén . . . dé*], someone gets drunk [*methúei*, the third person singular present active indicative of *methúō* {3184}, to get drunk]" (a.t.). The word *hós* (3739), one, is repeated twice, and it is the nominative singular masculine relative pronoun. We have one person going hungry, while another person is getting drunk. He who was refused food brought by those who had plenty went hungry in public, just as he did in private. And those who had plenty to eat and drink went to the extreme and drank so much that they got drunk. However, this was now being done in public where the needy could see their gluttony. This clearly illustrates the behavior of a greedy person. Unashamedly, they would exhibit their greed and selfishness at a love feast of all places. Their private lives showed in public, and they did not care. However, such should not be the behavior of the believer. The love feast did not last, because it did not produce the evidence of love. Rather, it became an occasion for scandal and shame and an exhibition of selfishness and lack of concern for others.

LESSONS:

1. The love feasts were also attended by unbelievers who took the opportunity to get together in the church to have a good time, demonstrating the selfish characteristics of their unregenerated nature.
2. Christians should not tolerate such a thing in church. This is why this practice in Corinth was short-lived, for it became a blemish to the Christian church.
3. A selfish person in private will show selfishness and greed in public.
4. If such a thing is allowed in the church, it gives the church a bad reputation in the community and brings shame on the name of Christ.

1 Cor. 11:22 | Christians Should Guard the Local Church

By no means! Do you not have houses in which to eat and to drink? Or do you despise the church of God and bring shame upon those who have nothing? What shall I say to you? Shall I praise you in this? I absolutely do not praise you.

The behavior of some of the Corinthians was reprehensible not only because it showed no concern for the needy among them and did not consider its influence on others, but it also maligned the testimony of the local church where their love feasts took place. While they were called "love feasts," it seems they were anything but. They seemed, rather, to be an exhibition of greed and gluttony and selfishness resembling the feasts in the idol temple.

"By No Means! Do You Not Have Houses in Which to Eat and Drink?"

Paul directs this question toward selfish people who have no concern for the image they project of the corporate life of the church. In Greek, this verse contains two negatives; it begins with *mḗ gár* (*mḗ* [3361], the relative "not" which expects a negative answer to the question that follows and *gár* [1063], therefore). I have chosen to translate this phrase as "By no means!"

Actually, this verse is the conclusion of Paul's previous remarks. "By no means! Do you not have houses [*ouk* {3756}, the absolute negative with the consonant *k* because the next word begins with a vowel, used here to negate the verbal idea; *échete* {2192}, you have, the second person plural present active indicative of the verb *échō*; *oikías*, the accusative plural feminine noun of *oikía* {3614}, residences] in which to eat and drink [*esthíein*, the present active infinitive of *esthíō* {2068}, to eat; *pínein*, the present active infinitive of *pínō* {4095}, to drink]?" (a.t.).The answer to be expected is, No, of course we are not without private residences in which we can eat and drink.

The Corinthians considered what and how much they ate and drank to be a private matter, even if they were eating in public. If others did not have as much as they did, that was their problem. But should they think only of themselves? When they came to church, they should have thought of their behavior and what impression it would leave on others, and with a view to sharing what they had, should have thought also of others who had no food and drink.

"Or Do You Despise the Church of God"

These Corinthians who engaged in the love feasts did not think of the effect their behavior might have on the church as a whole. Their love feasts were reminiscent of the feasts and orgies that took place in the idol temples and may have been carried over from that. Paul considered the church in Corinth to be a church that belonged to God in spite of all its faults and the wrong influences and impressions it exhibited. There were those who were joined to it to fulfill their selfish purposes and use it as an opportunity to show their affluence. However, it was still the church of God, for in it were true believers who belonged to the body of Christ, although their philosophies and practices were contrary to Paul's teaching. Any person associated with a local church of God must ask himself if he is in any way harming the impression of that for which the church of God stands. Will an improper attitude or behavior or dress be attributed to all the selfless people who are genuine members of the body of Christ?

The verb "despise" is *kataphroneíte*, the second person plural present active indicative of *kataphronéō* (2706), to hold in contempt, from *katá* (2596), against (thus denoting evil), and the basic verb *phronéō* (5426), to think. We despise God and His church when we do not consider others or do for them what God would have us do.

In the community of believers and unbelievers alike, there are two classes: those who have enough to comfortably sustain their lives and those who do not. Those who have enough are called "rich" (*ploúsioi* [4145]), and those who do not are called "poor" (*ptōchoí* [4434], poor to the point of the necessity of being helped by others if they are going to survive). The Lord said to the rich young ruler, "Sell whatsoever you have, and give to the poor, and you shall have treasure in heaven" (Mark 10:21). In the apostolic church, the first duty that believers recognized was helping the poor (Acts 2:44, 45, cf. 4:32, 34, 35). In the church of Jerusalem, seven were appointed to carry out the ministrations of the church to the poor widows of the community (Acts 6:1–4). In the letters of Paul, we have frequent references to the obligation to help the poor (Rom. 12:13; Eph. 4:28; 1 Tim. 6:18). In some of Paul's letters, we find him especially occupied with the collections which were being made for the poor Christians in Jerusalem (Gal. 2:10; Rom. 15:25, 26; 1 Cor. 16:1, 2; 2 Cor. 9:8, 9). In 1 John 3:17 we read, "Whoever has this world's goods, and beholds his brother in need, and shuts up his bowels of compassion from him, how does the love of God dwell in him?" John states that it is impossible to love God without loving one's brother (1 John 4:20).

"And Bring Shame Upon Those Who Have Nothing?"

But what were the rich doing as they came to the love feasts in the Corinthian church? Our verse addresses them saying that not only did they despise the church of God, but they "bring shame upon those who have nothing." The verb is *kataischúnete*, the second person plural present active indicative of *kataischúnō* (2617), to bring shame upon. This is the third time this verb is used in this chapter. In verse 4, we read, "Every man praying or prophesying, having his head covered, dishonors [*kataischúnei*] his head." The second time the verb occurs is in verse 5 and concerns the woman: "But every woman that prays or prophesies with her head uncovered dishonors [*kataischúnei*] her head: for that is even all one as if she were shaven." The third mention of the verb is here and is addressed to the rich as bringing shame upon the poor instead of helping them. By openly displaying their wealth, the rich caused the poor to be humiliated. It indicated a total disregard for them or their needs. They may have been homeless and utterly needy. What the rich did, in this instance, was to eat to satiety and drink to the point of drunkenness while the poor and hungry stood by and watched. This is why we branded these Corinthians in the church as unbelievers or thoughtless, for only an unbeliever or a thoughtless "Christian" would act in such a totally inconsiderate manner.

"What Shall I Say to You? Shall I Praise You in This?"

And then Paul expressed his indignation by posing the third question: "What shall I say to you?" And his answer is still another question: "Shall I praise you in this?" He uses the verb *epainésō*, the first person singular aorist active subjunctive of *epainéō* (1867), to praise. Shall I praise you for coming to church to feast while you completely disregard others who are there, and who have absolutely nothing?

In regard to this subject, our readers would do well to review our exegesis of verse 2. In that verse, Paul tells the Corinthians that whereas they do remember him, they must hold fast to the traditions as he had delivered them. Another time he used the word *epainéō* (praise) in a negative way was found in verse 17, and it is in this general context that their gathering together was for the worse, and not the better. The Corinthians came together to eat in church, but in doing so, they demonstrated how selfish they were and how they despised the church of God and brought shame upon the poor, whom the Lord so often commended (Luke 6:20, 24) even as He condemmed the inconsiderate rich.

"I Absolutely Do Not Praise You"

And the final word is, "I absolutely do not [*ouk*, the absolute negative which we included in the translation] praise you" (a.t.). The word *epainṓ*, praise, is in the present indicative, and it is used for the fourth time in this chapter.

<u>LESSONS</u>:

1. When unbelievers use the church for reasons other than hearing the gospel, it is usually for the worse and not for the better (v. 17).
2. Paul takes the liberty to chide the Corinthians because of their inconsiderate activity within the church.
3. He tells them that it would be better to practice this selfishness and greed at home, rather than in the church where it brought shame within and without.
4. It is inevitable that, in the church, there are those who are poor, and they should not be humiliated by anyone. Rather they should be helped materially and be lifted up to a position of dignity.
5. In this verse, as in verses 2 and 17, Paul repeats that there is pitifully little for which he can praise them.

1 Cor. 11:23 | A Celebration as Delivered by Christ

But I, myself, accurately received from the Lord that which I also faithfully delivered to you, that the Lord Jesus, in the night in which He was delivering Himself, received bread.

What originally began as a remembrance of the Lord's last supper with His disciples and of His death and resurrection became known in Corinth as love feasts. These love feasts, however, eventually degenerated into meals where the well-to-do ate their fill and drank to excess in the presence of others who were hungry. They showed no concern to meet the need of the poor, and shame was brought on both the needy and the name of Christ.

"But I, Myself, *Accurately* Received from the Lord"

This verse begins with *egṓ* (1473), I, myself. The "I received," however, could have been indicated simply by the suffix *on* of *parélabon*, the third person singular second aorist indicative of *paralambánō* (3880), to receive, but Paul chose to add emphasis by inserting the personal pronoun *egṓ*, I, myself. He thus stresses that he would not deliver to the Corinthians anything which he had not accurately received from the Lord. In Galatians 1:12 in writing about the gospel, he says, "For I neither received it of [*pará* {3844}] man, neither was I taught *it*, but by the revelation of Jesus Christ." We are therefore fully justified to translate the verb *parélabon* as "I accurately received."

Paul does not say that what he is about to describe he received personally from the hand of the Lord, but that the origin was from Him. Paul asserts that it was not changed from what it was when first received. The preposition that is used in the text is *apó* (575), from, denoting the historical source. On page 219, in my *Complete Word Study Dictionary: New Testament* in section V under the word *apó*, I have the following comment:

> Paul's use of *apó* in 1 Corinthians 11:23, "For I have received of [*apó*] the Lord," indicates that the institution of the Lord's Supper was originally due to the Lord Himself. It does not mean that Paul claims that he directly received it from the Lord, but that it originated directly with the Lord. The reading of one manuscript with *pará*, which would indicate the immediate reception by Paul of this tradition, must be rejected in view of the fact that Paul did not receive this directly from the Lord. Paul emphasizes that this ordinance of the Lord's Supper did not come to him through intermediaries, but that he wanted the Corinthians to realize that this ordinance of the Lord's Supper was something which originated with the Lord. He emphasizes only that which can be traced directly.

Verse 23 affirms the event in the life of the Lord Jesus that Paul claims to have received accurately and to have faithfully transmitted. We inserted in this verse in italics the adverb "accurately" which tells us how Paul received the information that he is about to convey to the Corinthians. This verb is also prefixed with the preposition *pará*, indicating personal reception. However, Paul did not receive it directly from the Lord because, in spite of the fact that he rightfully claims apostleship, he was not present on the night the first Lord's Supper was celebrated.

The word *parélabon* occurs for the first time in Paul's writing in this verse. In 2 Thessalonians 3:6, Paul says, "Now we command you [*paraggéllomen* {3853}; see the same verb used in

v. 17], brethren, in the name of our Lord Jesus Christ, that you withdraw yourselves from every brother that walks disorderly, and not after the tradition [*parádosin* {3862}] which he received [*parélabe* {TR}, received directly and accurately] of [*pará*] us." They were walking in a disorderly manner, not accurately as they had received directly (*pará*) the tradition from Paul. So, you see, if the traditions were not accurately followed as they were given by the Apostle Paul, they became a disorderly walk.

"That Which I Also *Faithfully* Delivered to You"

We chose to translate *hó*, the accusative singular neuter relative pronoun of *hós* (3739), as "that which," for if we translated it as "what," it could possibly indicate the plural, which it is not. Paul speaks about a single event, an institution that was set up for the Christian church to regularly commemorate. "Also" translated *kaí* (2532), and, which refers to that which he accurately received and faithfully delivered. We have translated the verb *parédōka*, the first person singular aorist active indicative of *paradídōmi* (3860), I deliver, as "I *faithfully* delivered." It is exactly the same verb as we find in the second verse of this chapter. There is the preposition *pará*, from, as a prefix which we chose to translate with the adverb "faithfully." This means that as Paul had accurately received it, so he faithfully delivered it to the Corinthian Christians.

Let us examine carefully these two words which are found in verse 2: *parédōka*, the first person singular aorist active indicative of *paradídōmi*, to personally deliver; and the noun *paradóseis*, the accusative plural of *parádosis*, tradition. Both words have the word *pará*, from or beside, which is a preposition denoting the greatest possible proximity. The verb means "faithfully delivered" and the noun means "traditions," thus that which was faithfully delivered. We have also taken the verb *katéchete* (2722) as the second person plural present active imperative, and not as the indicative, as it is usually taken by interpreters. This is an imperative. It is a command that Paul gives to the Corinthians to hold fast to the traditions that he delivered to them and as he delivered them, with no changes.

"That the Lord Jesus, in the Night in Which He Was Delivering Himself, Received Bread"

The verb which we have translated "delivering Himself" is *paredídoto*, the third person singular imperfect passive indicative of *paradídōmi*, to deliver myself. Although the verb is passive, it has a middle meaning, that is, "I was delivering myself."

Very clearly we see in the New Testament that it was neither Pilate nor the enemies of Christ who delivered Jesus to be crucified, but He delivered Himself, for they could not have done so had it not been by His permissive will. Paul, in Galatians 2:20, leaves no doubt that the Lord delivered Himself to be crucified for us: "I am crucified with Christ: nevertheless I live; yet not I, but Christ lives in me: and the life which I now live in the flesh, I live by the faith of the Son of God, who loved me and **gave Himself** for me." The verb translated here "gave Himself" is *paradóntos*, the genitive singular masculine second aorist active participle of *paradídōmi*. The translation is exactly correct, that He gave Himself. Also Ephesians 5:2 makes it clear that the delivery was active and voluntary: "And walk in love, as Christ also has loved us, and has **given Himself** for us an offering and a sacrifice to God for a sweet smelling savor." And in verse 25, it says, "Husbands, love your wives, even as Christ also loved the church, and **gave Himself** for it."

"He Received Bread"

The verb is *élaben*, the third person singular second aorist active indicative of *lambánō* (2983), to receive. The night that the Lord ate supper with His Twelve Disciples (Luke 22:14), He used the bread that provided the substance of the meal to indicate His body. It was a meal in celebration of the Passover (Mark 14:12), and the crucifixion of the Lord was to take place the next day. This represented an act of the greatest liberation of all—that of sinners from the bondage of sin. Passover was the most important Hebrew feast and an annual festival. It commemorated the final plague on Egypt when the firstborn of the Egyptians died and the Israelites were spared because of the blood applied to their doorposts (Ex. 12:11, 21, 27, 43, 48). The Passover was also called the "Feast of Unleavened Bread" (Ex. 23:15; Deut. 16:16), because only unleavened bread was eaten during the seven days immediately following. Unleavened bread was used because the people had no time to put leaven in their dough before their hasty departure from Egypt.

During New Testament times, large crowds gathered in Jerusalem to observe this annual celebration. Jesus and His disciples ate the Passover meal together on the eve of His death. During this meal, Jesus said, "This is my body," and "This cup is the new testament in My blood" (Luke 22:19, 20). The New Testament identifies Christ with the Passover sacrifice: "For even Christ our Passover is sacrificed for us" (1 Cor. 5:7). The bread that was on the table which Jesus and the Twelve Disciples ate during this Passover festival was unleavened bread (Lev. 23:4–8). Unleavened bread was symbolic to the Israelites to beware of corruptive influences (Ex. 12:14–20), for we find in the New Testament that leaven is symbolic of any evil influence which, if allowed to remain, can corrupt the body of believers. Jesus warned His disciples against the leaven of the Pharisees, that is, their teaching and hypocrisy (Matt. 16:5–12; Luke 12:1). Paul urged the Corinthians to remove wickedness from their midst and become fresh dough, unleavened loaves of sincerity and truth (1 Cor. 5:6–13). Jesus likely followed the tradition of celebrating Passover with bread that was unleavened, showing that He did not object to keeping traditions which were symbolic of essential lessons to which His followers needed to pay attention and adhere to.

The word for "bread" is *árton*, the accusative singular masculine noun of *ártos* (740), bread. Bread at that time had the appearance of a disk (Judg. 7:13), about one-half inch thick and twelve inches in diameter. Sometimes it was heart-shaped (2 Sam. 13:6, 8, 10). Bread was broken or torn, not cut, and was used as a staple in the Jewish diet. The word "bread" was used by the Lord Jesus to indicate that He was the Bread of Life (John 6:32, 33, 35). It is only proper that our Lord should have used unleavened bread to indicate His body, for He had no sin (Heb. 4:15).

The Lord Jesus wanted His disciples and the whole world to realize that as the Passover was the feast of liberation from Egypt, so His sacrifice on the cross symbolized His coming into the world and sacrificing Himself so that man may be free from sin. In the sixth chapter of John, after feeding thousands of people with five loaves of bread and two fishes, the Lord gave the great discourse on who He really was. Among other things, He referred to Himself as being the "Bread of Life" (v. 48). As John 1:4 states, "In Him was life, and the life was the light of men." The Lord Jesus did not come to this earth to give physical life, but spiritual life, which is the life of God. In order to procure that for anyone who would believe, He became flesh (John 1:14) which He gave for the world as a sacrifice for the sins of mankind (Eph. 1:7; Col. 1:14; Heb. 9:22). He Himself said, "I am the bread of life: he that comes to Me shall never hunger; and he that believes on Me shall never thirst" (John 6:35). Jesus was not a common man, for He was unique in that He was born of a virgin (Luke 1:26–37). Jesus Christ proved that He was a unique Savior through His resurrection. He came as a human being, yet without sin, to die for mankind's sin and to rise from the dead.

He thus proved that He was all that He claimed to be. In John 6:51, He said, "I am the living bread which came down from heaven: if any man eat of this bread, he shall live forever; and the bread that I will give is My flesh which I will give for the life of the world." The Lord Jesus asserted the truth that He is the "Bread of Life," the bread that gives life, and He gives life to anyone who eats of it. This eating of the bread, however, is not the actual eating of His flesh as some believe, but it is believing in Him as the only hope of eternal life for the sinner. However, in none of Christ's teachings did He intimate or imply that by the actual eating of bread we might experience a spiritual transformation of life. John 3:16 puts it very clearly, that he who **believes** on Him should not perish but have eternal life.

LESSONS:

1. Paul affirmed that that which came down to him from the Lord was accurately received and faithfully delivered by him.
2. In reality, nobody imposed death on the Lord Jesus, but He willingly delivered Himself to die for our sins.
3. He took the bread that was used for the Passover meal to represent His own body that He was going to sacrifice for the sins of the world.
4. Throughout Scripture, leaven indicates sin, and so it was only proper that Christ used unleavened bread to represent His body since He had no sin.

1 Cor. 11:24 | *How and Why the Lord's Supper Is Celebrated*

> *And having given thanks, He broke it and said, "Take, eat; this is My body that is being broken for you; this keep doing in My remembrance."*

The Lord Jesus Christ had delivered Himself to be sacrificed for the sins of the world. It was He Himself who instituted the Lord's Supper in order that believers might not forget from whence came their redemption. What started out as a solemn remembrance of our Lord's sacrifice degenerated into a feast of gluttony and drunkenness in Corinth. Paul is calling the Corinthians back to the sacred purpose of the Lord's Table.

"And Having Given Thanks,"

When the Lord received the bread that was on the table where He ate with His disciples, He gave thanks (*eucharistḗsas*, the nominative singular masculine aorist active participle of *eucharistéō* [2168], to give thanks, derived from *eu* [2095], well, good, and *charízomai* [5483], to grant, give). The word for "thanks" has in it *cháris* (5485), grace, which means undeserved favor. This is the participle that Luke 22:19 uses, while Matthew 26:26 and Mark 14:22 has the participle *eulogḗsas*, the nominative singular masculine aorist active participle of *eulogéō* (2127), to speak well of, which is derived from *eu*, well, good, as in *eucharistéō*; and *lógos* (3056), word. *Eulogéō* means to bless or to speak well of. But invoking God's Word is invoking His action, His will. *Eucharistéō* means to thank or to recognize that there is goodness in the will of God in imparting His grace (*cháris*). So basically, these two verbs, *eucharistéō*, to give thanks, and *eulogéō*, to bless, mean one and the same thing. They are a recognition of the grace of God which is undeserved favor, and an invitation to the Lord to speak well or to act well in our lives. The same applies to the noun *eucharistía* (2169), gratitude or thankfulness, for whatever comes upon the Christian is the result of the grace of God, and that grace is always undeserved and therefore we should be thankful for it. Well has the whole celebration of the death of Christ been named in church history as Holy Communion because "Eucharist" means thanksgiving. The grace of God is shown in our participation of the undeserved favor of God. Holy Communion is not for us to receive the grace of God, but for us to acknowledge the personal experience of grace already possessed. That is why Paul, in 1 Corinthians 10:16, refers to the cup of the Holy Communion as "the cup of blessing" (*eulogías*) of God, for He has spoken favorably to us in making His will of forgiveness known through His sacrifice on our behalf. In the same verse, Paul speaks about the fellowship (*koinōnía* [2842], fellowship, partnership, participation) of the body of Christ. The word "communion" that we use in Holy Communion is *koinōnía*. So either the verb *eucharistéō* (to give thanks) or *eulogéō* (to bless) is appropriate in the consecration of the actual bread that the Lord took in His hands.

We do not know the words of thanksgiving or of blessing that the Lord Jesus offered to His Father as He took the bread. Although Paul does not tell us the exact words, we know Christ's intent. Through His thanksgiving, He expressed His perfect agreement with the Father regarding His coming crucifixion for the remission of the sins of the world. When the Lord Jesus thanked His Father, He always indicated that what He was doing was in perfect agreement with the will of the Father. It is significant to note that Jesus always gave thanks to His Father, never others. Whenever Jesus thanked the Father, He blessed Him that, as the God-Man, He could confess His total agreement of purpose and achievement with the Father. When the Lord Jesus, with two fishes and five loaves of bread, fed 5,000 men and an unknown number of women and children, we read in Matthew 14:19 that He took the five loaves and two fishes, and He looked up into heaven and blessed them (*eulógēse*), and He broke them and gave them to His disciples. When He was about to feed the 4,000 with the seven loaves of bread and a few fish, He gave thanks (*eucharistḗsas*) and broke them, and gave to His disciples, and the disciples to the multitude (Matt. 15:36; Mark 8:6). Whom did Jesus thank? His Father with whom His relationship was unique.

The event of the establishment of the celebration of the Lord's Supper took place on a Thursday night. On Friday came Gethsemane which is described in Matthew 26:36–56; Mark 14:32–42; Luke 22:39–54, and John 18:1–11. When He met with His disciples to make them participants of the bread that symbolized His body and the cup of blessing, He, as the God-Man, thanked the Father. The God in Him knew absolutely that He was going to die and that His death was going to provide grace for everyone who would believe and appropriate it as an act of God's reconciliation (2 Cor. 5:17–21). When Christ thanked God His Father for the cup that represented His blood that He was going to shed for sinners, He expressed His full, divine agreement with God the Father's purpose. Christ's physical death was necessary, for only through a sinless sacrifice could provision be made for the remission of the sins of man. But when it came to the actual giving of His sinless body (Heb. 4:15), the

Lord Jesus expressed a natural dread regarding the horrible death He was about to endure: "O, My Father, if it be possible, let this cup pass from Me; nevertheless, not as I will, but as You will" (Matt. 26:39; Mark 14:35, 36; Luke 22:42). It is beyond our human capacity to know what went on between God the Father and God the Son within His eternal purpose to achieve our salvation. However, it is for us as humans to realize that in the incarnation and crucifixion of Christ, His bodily sacrifice on the cross was not without the agony of the flesh. Thus, we find God the Son communicating with God the Father, knowing that man's reconciliation had to be through physical sacrifice, for that was the very purpose of the incarnation. Our Lord was incarnated not only to display a life of miracles and divine words, but to die a purposeful death. In Matthew 26:26 and Mark 14:22, we have the verb "bless" (*eulogḗsas*) while in Luke 22:17, 19, we have the word "to give thanks" (*eucharistḗsas*). The two words are used synonymously to express the means by which the grace of God can come upon individuals who believe. We can speak well of God, realizing that His grace liberated us from sin, requiring a great sacrifice beyond our ability to comprehend.

"He Broke It"

While *eucharistḗsas* or *eulogḗsas* tells of the consecration of the bread that the Lord took in His hand, the next words "broke it" (*éklase*, the third person singular aorist active indicative of *kláō* [2806], to break) implies breaking it into smaller pieces for the purpose of distributing it. The bread symbolized the body of Jesus, and those who experience His salvation must realize that it was necessary for the body of Jesus Christ to be broken in order to procure our salvation. Whereas Christ's death was for all mankind, it must be individually appropriated. Christ's spotless and holy body was given as a sacrifice for the complete and eternal salvation of individuals (Heb. 9:12).

We find the verb "break" (*kláō*) used when the Lord performed the miracle of feeding the multitude of over 5,000 (Matt. 14:19; Mark 8:19) and when He fed another group of over 4,000 (Matt. 15:38; Mark 8:6). He broke the bread and the fish so that each one participating in these miracles might be fully and personally satisfied. He did the same thing during the first Communion when He thanked the Father for the sufficiency of His grace for all. "He broke," then, has the meaning of distributing Himself, and that distribution of Himself was sufficient for the full satisfaction of individuals.

In the feeding of the 5,000 and the 4,000, not only is the verb *kláō,* break, used in reference to the bread and fish, but also the verb *chortázō* (5526), to fill, satisfy (Matt. 14:20; 15:37; Mark 6:42; 8:4, 8). Similarly, in the distribution of Jesus Christ Himself there is full satisfaction for each individual who partakes. Spiritually speaking, the Lord Jesus fully satisfies everyone who comes to Him and asks for forgiveness. His grace also is more than enough for the full satisfaction of all.

In both instances of the Lord Jesus feeding the multitudes, not only was everyone satisfied with Christ's distribution of bread and fish, but large quantities were left over. The word that describes the left-over bread and fish is *perisseúon*, the accusative singular neuter present active participle of *perisseúō* (4052), to abound (Matt. 14:20; 15:37). In the distribution of Christ's grace not only is every individual satisfied fully, but also His grace abounds to share with others. The spiritual applications from the physical events are beautiful indeed.

"And Said, 'Take, Eat"

Jesus shared the bread that was available on the table and urged His disciples to "Take, eat" (*lábete*, the second person plural second aorist active imperative of *lambánō* [2983], to take; *phágete*, the second person plural second aorist active imperative of *esthíō* {2068}, to eat). This was a specific command to the disciples, although it was the common bread which was part of their evening meal in celebration of the Passover. The same bread which they enjoyed for their evening meal was used by the Lord to symbolize His body which would be crucified for their sins. The Lord does not speak thus to those who have no experience of believing on Him, but to His disciples only. Their involvement in receiving and eating the bread that He was now offering them involved faith in believing that it symbolized His own body. The taking and eating of the bread did not produce faith, but required faith in the Person of Jesus Christ who spoke the words, "Take, eat."

The expression "breaking of bread" in Acts 2:42, 46 may refer to the breaking of bread at the institution of the Lord's Supper, but we cannot be sure that it refers only to that. What is significant, however, is that all who partook of the bread were believers, for it tells us that "all that believed were together, and had all things in common" (v. 44). Faith is what made the participation in the breaking of the bread possible and significant. To unbelievers, the words of Christ, "This is My body," would be totally meaningless.

"This Is My Body"

What was the Lord implying when He said, "This is my body"? First, He meant to say that as the bread was an actual, physical substance, so was His body which was given for those who believe in spiritual sustenance. We read in John 1:14 that He that dwelt in the physical body of Jesus was the Word (*Lógos*) who had been with the Father eternally (John 1:1–3), for "the Word became flesh" (John 1:14). He who was from the beginning became flesh (*sárx* [4561]). A real body cannot physically exist without blood, for as Leviticus 17:11 says, "The life of the flesh is in the blood." John 1:14 states that the Word became flesh and tabernacled (*eskḗnōsen*, the third person singular aorist active indicative of *skēnóō* [4637], to tabernacle, live in a tent) among us. This was Jesus Christ who took upon Himself a physical, earthly but still special (Heb. 2:14) body which was crucified outside the gates of Jerusalem (Mark 15:20–47; Col. 1:22; Heb. 13:11, 12). And why is our earthly body called a "tent"? Because a tent is quickly and easily torn down and moved elsewhere. It is only a temporary habitation as are our earthly bodies.

The bread that the Lord told the disciples to take and eat was obviously not His actual body, but symbolized the body that He was going to give to be crucified for the redemption of mankind. The Word indwelt the physical body that all could see and hear (1 John 1:1) and that could be crucified for everybody to witness. It was the Spirit (John 4:24) who became visible to all so that it could be said of Him that He died for our sins, and that He was buried, and that He arose the third day according to the Scriptures, and that He was seen by the disciples and a multitude of believers. Through the crucifixion of Christ, resurrection may become verifiable (1 John 1:1–3), to which verification Paul devotes 1 Corinthians 15.

"That Is Being Broken"

When our Lord spoke these words, His crucifixion had not yet taken place, but the process involving His death was taking place at the time that He asked His disciples to take and eat the bread that symbolized His body. Matthew 26:26 and Mark 14:22 present the Lord as having said, "Take, eat, this is My body." Luke 22:19, however, says, "He broke it and gave to them, saying, 'This is My body which is being given [*didómenon*, the nominative singular neuter present passive participle of *dídōmi* {1325}, to give, which can only be translated correctly as "is being given"] for you.' " This expresses the purpose for which

He took upon Himself a body. The giving of His body was an event and point in history the purpose of which, however, had no limit in time and space. It was a historical event of eternal value and purpose.

When we come to 1 Corinthians 11:24, we find that the Textus Receptus and the Majority Text have the participle *klṓmenon*, meaning "which is broken," the nominative singular neuter present passive participle of *kláō*, to break. The present participle here has the same significance as the present participle found in Luke 22:19, *didómenon*, the one being given, which takes the application and the purpose of it beyond the limitations of history. We prefer the inclusion of *klṓmenon*, "which is broken," in our text (which is rejected by the critical texts), because it fits perfectly with *didómenon* which is included in all the texts.

"For You"

The crucifixion of the Lord Jesus which was yet to come on the following day, Friday noon, is explained as being "for you" (*hupér* [5228]). The primary meaning of *hupér* is "over," a preposition meaning "for the benefit" or "representation" (John 11:50; 18:14). Here it means that Christ died in place of the believers dying for their own sins. He could die to take away man's sin because He was sinless (Heb. 4:15). The preposition portrays a vicarious and redemptive purpose. Instead of the sinner dying himself and being condemned forever because of his sin, Christ died in the sinner's place that He might give him the opportunity to escape death by exercising faith in His sacrifice.

In 1 Corinthians 11:24 the "you" in the phrase "for you" means effectively for the believers, that is, for you who have believed on Christ and who are to partake of the Lord's Supper in remembrance of what He did to redeem you from your sins.

There are some who believe that Christ died only for those who effectively believe on Him unto salvation. This is known as limited atonement and is based on Mark 14:24: "This is My blood of the New Testament, which is shed **for many.**" The word *pollṓn*, the genitive plural masculine adjective of *polús* (4183), much, shows us that no matter how many believe, they are included in the number of those for whom Christ effectively died. But we must also stress that Paul emphasizes that Christ died "**for all.**" This is affirmed in 2 Corinthians 5:14: "For the love of Christ constrains us; because we thus judge, that if One died **for all**, then were all dead"; and in 1 Timothy 2:6, "Who gave Himself a ransom **for all**, to be testified in due time." As far as the historical event of the death of Christ is concerned, it took place once-for-all for as many as believe effectively and all potentially. Hebrews 9:28 says, "So Christ was once offered to bear the sins of many; and unto them that look for Him shall He appear the second time without sin unto salvation." It is impossible that Christ should die again for human sin. First Peter 3:18 says, "For Christ also has once [*hápax* {530}, one time numerically] suffered for sins, the Just for the unjust, that He might bring us to God, being put to death in the flesh, but quickened in the Spirit."

Though the death of Christ was a historical event as His incarnation was, yet the purpose for which He was born and died has no historical limitation until He returns at His Second Coming. Paul touches upon this in verse 26 in full agreement with what we find in Matthew 26:29, Mark 14:25, and Luke 22:18.

"This Keep Doing"

Paul tells us that we must celebrate the effective result of the death of Christ upon the cross by continuing to remember this event. "This keep doing [*toúto* {5124}, the nominative singular neuter demonstrative pronoun of *hoútos* {3778}, this one, meaning 'This which I have just done'; *poieíte*, keep doing, the second person plural present active imperative of *poiéō* {4160}, to do]" (a.t.). The present imperative has the meaning in Luke 22:19 of "Start doing it and keep on doing it." But in 1 Corinthians 11:24, the disciples were already commemorating their Lord's death, so it only means to keep on doing it. The only other verse where we find this command expressed is in 1 Corinthians 11 verse 25, and here it should be translated "this keep on doing." It is interesting, indeed, that these are the only three passages in which we find this command to start doing or start celebrating the Lord's Supper, and it is to be continued until He who initiated the age of grace comes back to terminate it (1 Cor. 11:26).

"In My Remembrance"

What was the real purpose of celebrating the Lord's Supper? Paul quotes from the Lord's express command, "in My remembrance" (a.t.). The "in" is the translation of the preposition of *eis* (1519), for the purpose of, with the goal of. It denotes the spiritual result of the celebration of the Lord's Supper by Christians. The word "remembrance" is *anámnēsin*, the accusative singular feminine noun from *anámnēsis* (364) from the verb *anamimnḗskō* (363), to remind. We need to constantly be reminded lest we forget what it cost Jesus Christ to redeem us from our sins. The only other place that the word "remembrance" is mentioned, besides Luke 22:19 and 1 Corinthians 11:24, 25, is Hebrews 10:3: "But in those sacrifices there is a remembrance again made of sins every year." The Apostle knows how easy it is for us to forget the seriousness of our sins, and the terrible sacrifice offered for those sins was a reminder of the hideousness of our sin. We are in constant danger, as Hebrews 10:2 states, to have "no more conscience of sins." Therefore, the sacrifices for sins before Christ's death should arouse in us also the consciousness of sins and the cost of redemption in and through Christ. Thus one reason the celebration of the Lord's

Supper should be enacted by us faithfully is so that we may not lose the ever-present awareness of sin. If this spiritual result of the celebration of the Lord's Supper is not evident and predominant, then it is useless. People who have not been redeemed cannot gain any spiritual value by participating in the physical act of receiving and eating of the Communion bread. This applies generally to all the teachings of Christ. Doing something that does not require repentance and faith merely to gain favor with God cannot have a spiritual effect on us.

It is indeed significant that the Lord's Supper would remind us of Christ. The three verses where the phrase occurs (Luke 22:19; 1 Cor. 11:24, 25) do not say "in remembrance of My death," but "of Me" (*eis tḗn emḗn*, in my, the accusative singular feminine first person possessive pronoun referring to the feminine noun *anámnēsis*, remembrance). Why did the Lord say, "In My remembrance" and not "In remembrance of My death"? The answer is found in that death could not hold Him prisoner. The Lord wants us to remember His crucifixion, but above all, that He rose again and is living to indwell us that we may be members of His body, the church. There is no event that occurred to Jesus Christ greater than His resurrection, but the crucifixion was the way whereby He paid the penalty for our sins. Through His resurrection, He could show His glory and power, that all authority in heaven and on earth was given to Him (Matt. 28:18).

LESSONS:

1. The two words used by the Lord in the establishment of the celebration of the Lord's Supper are the verbs *eucharistéō* (2168), to thank, and *eulogéō* (2127), to bless, which essentially mean the same thing, for one contains the grace (*cháris* [5485]) of God and the other the Word (*Lógos* [3056]) of God. They are both prefixed with the adjective or adverb *eu* (2095), good or well.

2. God's grace and Word as expressed and spoken are sufficient for each one individually and for all.
3. The death of Christ occurred on the cross once-and-for-all, but it has an effect on humanity as a whole for eternity. Those who repent and believe receive eternal life, and those who do not believe receive eternal perdition (John 3:18–20; 1 Tim. 4:10).
4. The only limitation of time for the celebration of the Lord's Supper is the Age of Grace, from the moment of the death of Christ to the glorious time of His return.
5. Because we may forget what it cost Christ to redeem us from sin, the celebration of His death reminds us of the price He paid for our sins and the glorious life He lives in us (Rom. 8:10; 1 Cor. 12:13).

1 Cor. 11:25 | *Cup Participation Made Possible by Jesus' Blood*

> *In the same manner, also the cup, after they had eaten supper, saying, "This cup is the new testament in My blood. This keep doing every time you are to drink in My remembrance."*

The death of Christ on the cross was a once-and-for-all sacrifice for the sins of man. All who believe and accept this sacrifice for their sins will be saved. Since mankind loses the consciousness of sin and forgets the terrible cost of his redemption, he is commanded to partake of the Lord's Supper as a remembrance until Christ takes him unto Himself. Because this is a command of our Lord Jesus Christ, we will do well to study it carefully.

"In the Same Manner"

This whole phrase, "In the same manner," translates one word, the adverb *hōsaútōs* (5615). It is derived from *hōs* (5613), as; and *autós* (846), the same. It could also be translated "likewise." It means that what the Lord Jesus did with the bread, He also did with the cup. The phrase "He gave thanks," which is found in verse 24, is expressed in regard to the cup specifically in Matthew 26:27. It is also repeated in Mark 14:23 and Luke 22:17. In regard to the bread, however, in Mark 14:22, the Lord is said to have blessed (*eulogḗsas*, the nominative singular masculine aorist active participle of *eulogéō* [2127], to bless, to speak well of) it. This could be transliterated as to cause to intervene and act for the welfare of those who believed in what the broken body of Christ represented. The breaking of the body of the Lord Jesus denotes the enacting of the grace of God. The word *eucharistéō*, which means to thank, contains in it the word *cháris* (5485), grace. Its synonymous verb is *eulogéō* which is derived from *eu* (2095), good or well, and *Lógos* (3056), Word, which is the pre-existent name of Christ who became flesh (John 1:1, 14). The grace of God can come only upon the individual who accepts the transforming power of that grace through the incarnation of the Eternal Word.

"Also the Cup, after They Had Eaten Supper"

The Lord Jesus, in the night prior to His crucifixion, took the bread and said, "This is My body which is broken for you." Then He shared the cup with His disciples and said "This is my blood of the new testament, which is shed for many for the remission of sins." So the cup specifically represented His blood; nevertheless, His blood was part of His body. He spoke of His blood as accomplishing a unique function in the process of salvation.

The Lord was stressing to His disciples and to us that it was important to realize that the crucifixion meant two things. First, it referred to His physical death, and secondly, it referred to the shedding of the blood that flowed within the veins of His body for the redemption of mankind. In the three accounts of the celebration of the Lord's Supper (Matt. 26:28; Mark 14:24; Luke 22:20), the participle "being shed" (*ekchunómenon*, the nominative singular neuter present passive participle of *ekchéō* or *ekchúnō* [1632], to pour out) is used. The Lord Jesus could have died on the cross without shedding His blood, and He could have shed blood without dying, but we are told that He did both—He died and He shed His blood. We read in the Scriptures that Jesus died once for all (2 Cor. 5:15; Heb. 9:26, 27; 10:10; 1 Pet. 3:18). The present participial form of the verb *ekchunómenon* regarding the institution of the Lord's Supper is used to indicate not a continuous pouring out, but that the pouring out was before the foundation of the world, planned and destined to be so, not being chronologically limited as to its effectiveness. His blood was to be shed once and for all to accomplish the eternal cleansing from sin for all those who would believe (1 John 1:7).

Paul does not say with what the cup is filled. It is to be understood, however, that it was filled with "the fruit [*génēma* {MT}, produce, as contrasted with *génnēma* {1081}, offspring in the TR] of the vine [*ámpelos* {288}]," as Mark 14:25 says. The word *oínos* (3631), fermented wine, never occurs in the passages referring to the Lord's Supper or in this Corinthians passage. Simply it says, "This cup is the new testament in My blood." The cup represents the blood that Jesus shed on the cross.

The Lord's Supper, therefore, depicts two important things that took place when Jesus was going to die the next day: His body was to cease functioning in the normal physical way, and His blood was to be shed (Heb. 2:14). As I explain in a detailed article under the word "blood" (*haíma* [129]) in *The Complete Word Study Dictionary: New Testament* (pp. 92–96), Christ shed His blood which was accepted by the Father as full satisfaction of His righteousness (Rom. 5:1, 9; Heb. 9:12–14, 23–28). Through Jesus' death He brought about the reconciliation (*katallagḗ* [2643], atonement) between God and man (Rom. 5:11). The shedding of the blood of Christ provided the expiation (*hilasmós,* [2434]), the means whereby sin is covered and remitted objectively, the act of propitiation [1 John 2:2; 4:10; see *hilasmós*] in our above-mentioned Dictionary).

For the second time in this verse, the Apostle uses the definite article in front of the word "cup." It is "**the** cup" (*tó potḗrion*).

It was not just any cup, but the specific cup which had in it the fruit of the vine representing the blood of Christ which was shed on the cross. In 1 Corinthians 10:16 this is called "the cup of blessing which we bless." It is the cup which God has used to bring blessing to us, His intervention to redeem us from our helpless plight of sin. Not only did God speak well about what took place as a result of the sacrifice of Christ in bringing His grace to us, but we speak well of that which brought God's blessing to us. Paul extolls the effectiveness of the shedding of the blood by Christ. Only we who have experienced the grace of God can speak well of (*eulogoúmen*, we speak well of, we extol) that grace which is unknown and ignored by the world.

In 1 Corinthians 10:21 we find this cup called the "cup of the Lord" in contrast to the "cup of the demons" of which those feasting in idolatry partook.

That this is the "cup of blessing" only for believers whose sins have been cleansed by the blood of Christ is evident by the fact that John in Revelation 14:10 speaks of another cup: His wrath (*thumós* [2372], outburst of anger) and the cup of His indignation (*orgḗs*, the genitive of *orgḗ* [3709]) which pertains to God's abhorrence of sin and the grief that accompanies it. John, in speaking of the eschatological judgment of God, says,

> The same shall drink of the wine [*oínou,* the genitive of *oínos,* wine, in contrast to the fruit of the vine as in Matt. 26:29 {*gennḗmatos,* TR, MT}; Mark 14:25 {*gennḗmatos,* TR; *genḗmatos,* MT}; Luke 22:18 {*gennḗmatos,* TR; *genḗmatos,* MT} used to represent the blood of Christ] of the wrath of God which is poured out without mixture into the cup of His indignation, and he shall be tormented with fire and brimstone in the presence of the holy angels, and in the presence of the Lamb.

It is significant, indeed, to see how the Lord Jesus who lived on earth in a sinless human body (Heb. 4:15), suffering and being sacrificed for our sins (2 Cor. 5:21), is going to show forth His anger and His indignation upon those who have refused to accept that sacrifice. Every person has the choice of facing Jesus as his or her Savior or one day facing Him as the final Judge because of his or her rejection of Christ's love and sacrifice. The same expression is used in Revelation 16:19. It is significant to note that the definite article is also in front of the noun "cup" in these two instances, reminding us of the judgment of God upon unbelievers.

"Saying, 'This Cup Is the New Testament in My Blood'"

That which the Lord Jesus was offering to His disciples in the cup represented His own blood. The expression "in my blood" in Greek is *en* (1722), in; *tṓ*, the dative singular neuter of *ho* (3588), the; *emṓ*, the dative singular neuter first person possessive pronoun of *emós* (1699), mine, used in an emphatic manner; *haímati*, the dative singular neuter of *haíma*, blood. It is the same as the Lord saying that His blood is different from that of any other human or creature (Heb. 2:14). It is unique. This is also indicated by the expression "new testament" (*kainḗ* [2537], qualitatively new; *diathḗkē* [1242], testament, will).

In order to distinguish the blood of Jesus Christ from the blood of anyone else, twice in Romans (3:25; 5:9), Paul uses the expression "In His own [*autoú*, the genitive singular neuter personal pronoun of *autós*, meaning His very own] blood" (a.t.). Unfortunately, the emphatic *autoú* is missing from most of the translations. The same is true with the translation of Ephesians 1:7. In Hebrews 13:11, 12 the differentiation is made between the blood of animals and His own (*idíou*, the genitive singular masculine adjective of *ídios* [2398], own) blood (cf. Heb. 9:12, 13). The blood referred to in 1 Corinthians 11:25 is the blood of Christ (1 Cor. 10:16; Eph. 2:13; Heb. 9:14; 1 Pet. 1:19), the blood of Jesus (Heb. 10:19), the blood of Jesus Christ (1 Pet. 1:2; 1 John 1:7), the blood of the Lord (1 Cor. 11:27), and the blood of His cross (Col. 1:20).

The blood of the Lord Jesus was unique in that it was not the blood derived from a female and a male. All the Greek manuscripts have the word "bloods" (the plural *haimátōn* and not the singular *haíma*) in John 1:13: "Who was born **not of bloods**, and not of the will of a husband." This word "bloods" does not refer to Jesus' blood as being derived from the bloods of a man and a woman. No other man was ever born of a virgin through the intervention of God the Holy Spirit. While the High Priest entered the Holy of Holies once a year to offer sacrifices (Heb. 9:25), the Lord Jesus entered once and for all (*ephápax* [2178], on one occasion only for all [Heb. 9:12]). He did not offer a sacrifice for His own sin and the sins of others as the High Priest did, but only for the sins of others since He was without sin (Heb. 4:15). Therefore, He could indeed say, as the Apostle Paul affirms, that it was the unique blood, His own blood, that He shed and that was able to satisfy the justice of God and provide redemption for all, specifically for those who believe (2 Cor. 5:15; 1 Tim. 2:4, 6; 4:10; Titus 2:11; 2 Pet. 3:9).

In Galatians 4:24, Paul speaks of two testaments (*diathḗkai*, the nominative plural feminine noun of *diathḗkē*, testament). In 2 Corinthians 3:14, we find the Old (*palaiá* [3820], not recent, prior one, old) Testament. This should be differentiated from *archaía* (744), original or primeval. Originally, the Lord created man and gave him the freedom to eat of all the trees of Paradise except one. Thus God would test man's fidelity and obedience (Gen. 3:1–13). But man disobeyed God and fell from the Almighty's favor. Consequent to the fall of man, he was given the Law from Mount Sinai which constituted the Old (*palaiá*) Testament. The New Testament is called *kainḗ*, new, fresh, qualitatively different. Although it is called *diathḗkē*, testament, it means that which was given by God Himself. The New Testament is a declaration of God's intentions and will. The verbal form is *diatíthemai* (1303) which means to declare one's intentions. A person prepares his will or testament which is to be effected upon his death. This is not a covenant between the author and his heirs, for in reality, the heirs have no say regarding the will. It is not an agreement or covenant between two parties, but a statement of the will of the one party. When God gave His testament to Moses, He regulated the conduct of Israel by laws pertaining to most aspects of life. It was not a "covenant" which would have been expressed with the word *sunthḗkē*, an agreement between two people or between God and man. This word does not occur at all in the New Testament. The word "testament" occurs thirty-three times in the New Testament: four times in the three synoptic Gospels, twice in Acts, nine times by Paul, seventeen times in Hebrews, and once in Revelation. In the Old Testament, it was a legal institution, and in the New Testament, it was the promise of redemption through the blood of Christ and hence liberation from the domination of sin. As far as the law was concerned, it promised God's reward for obedience and God's punishment for disobedience. In relation to the blood of Christ, however, which is the New Testament, it promised enslavery to Christ which, however, meant liberation from sin (Rom. 6:17–23). That is why the Lord said in Matthew 5:17, "Think not that I am come to destroy the law or the prophets: I am not come to destroy, but to fulfill." He who has experienced redemption from sin finds in the blood of Christ a voluntary slavery in which there is the greatest freedom possible. In Romans 11:27, the Lord said, "This is My testament [*diathḗkē*] unto them, when I shall take away their sins." And in Romans 9:4, Paul says, "Who are Israelites? To whom pertains the adoption, and the glory, and the testaments [*diathḗkai*, here equivalent to *epaggelíai* {1860}, promises or divine assurances of reaching the goal], and the giving of the law, and the service of God, and the promises." To accentuate the hope contained in God's testament to man, Paul writes in Ephesians

2:12, "At that time you were without Christ, being aliens from the commonwealth of Israel, and strangers from the testaments of promise [*epaggelías*], having no hope, and without God in the world." In Romans 10:4, Paul delineates that "Christ is the end [*télos* {5056}, the goal] of the law for righteousness to everyone that believes."

This qualitatively New (*kainē*) Testament which has been fulfilled in the coming of Christ has been accomplished by the shedding of the blood of Jesus Christ (Matt. 26:28; Mark 14:24; Luke 22:20; 1 Cor. 11:25). It is appropriated by faith only. Any outward manifestation of external symbolism and obedience to it is simply a confirmation of the appropriation of the grace of God by faith (Eph. 2:8–10). Nobody is saved by simply participating in the Lord's Supper and being baptized. These two ordinances which Christ established simply declare a person's confession that he has been saved by believing on the Lord Jesus Christ (John 3:16).

This testament that Christ gave us is not only qualitatively new (*kainḗ*), it is better. This we find in Hebrews 7:22; 8:6: "By so much was Jesus made a surety of a better [*kreíttonos*, the genitive singular feminine adjective of *kreíttōn* {2909}, better] testament"; "But now has He obtained a more excellent ministry, by how much also He is the mediator of a better testament, which was established upon better promises."

In 1 Corinthians 11:25 under study, the definite article *hē* is to be noted before "New Testament." It is not **a** New Testament, but **the** New Testament, the final promises of God on the indwelling of Christ. When we believe on the Lord Jesus Christ and appropriate the power resident in His blood, then we find redemption that is eternal (Heb. 9:12) and salvation that is everlasting (Heb. 5:9).

"This Keep Doing Every Time You Are to Drink in My Remembrance"

The same command regarding the bread applies to the participation of the cup: *toúto poieíte*, this keep doing. The length of time is designated in verse 26, "till He come."

How often this ordinance of the Lord's Supper should be observed is detailed by the adverb *hosákis* (3740) from *hósos* (3745), how great, how much, and the suffix *kis*, the numerical termination meaning "times." It means as many times as you do this, but it does not delineate how many times or how often. The adverb is followed by *án* (302), a particle denoting experiential supposition, that is, as many times as you celebrate what I have detailed. The verb that follows is *pínēte*, the second person plural present active subjunctive of *pínō* (4095), to drink, thus, every time you are to drink. It does not make any difference how often you partake of the cup, every time you do so you should do it to remember the Lord Jesus and His sacrifice for you. The expression denoting "in remembrance of Me" is exactly the same as in the previous verse concerning the bread. What we have said there also applies here.

<u>LESSONS</u>:

1. The Bible speaks of two testaments, the Old (*palaiá* [3820]) meaning previous to the present one, and the New (*kainḗ* [2537]) meaning qualitatively new.
2. The Old Testament concerned the giving of the Law to Moses on Mount Sinai, and the New Testament concerned the one initiated by the incarnation, the crucifixion, and the resurrection of Jesus in Jerusalem.
3. The New Testament is called "a better testament" (Heb. 8:6) because it is qualitatively better than the Old Testament.
4. Jesus Christ is the fulfillment of the Law (Matt. 5:17; Rom. 10:4).

5. The present Testament is "the New Testament," the last of the two through which the Lord made known to us His final plans (Gal. 4:24).

1 Cor. 11:26 | How Often and Long to Give the Lord's Supper

Whenever, therefore, if you are to eat this bread and to drink this cup, you clearly declare the death of the Lord during the time till He comes.

In the previous verses we have dealt with the elements of the Lord's Supper. This verse takes up the frequency and the extent of time we are to continue in this remembrance.

"Whenever, Therefore, if You Are to Eat This Bread and to Drink This Cup"

How often the Lord's Supper should be celebrated is left to the objective need of being reminded of the death of Christ. For the second time in 1 Corinthians 11, we find the adverb *hosákis* (3740), whenever or as often (vv. 25, 26). Each and every time we celebrate the Lord's Supper, we should clearly declare that it is a celebration which reminds us of the death of the Lord Jesus Christ.

The "therefore" which translates the Greek *gár* (1063) refers to the previous verses and concludes the reason for the celebration and participation in the bread and the cup. The two go together. If one participates only in the one element and not the other, it is not the Lord's Supper that is being celebrated.

Then follows the objective conjunction *án* (302) which is a contraction of *eán* (1437), if. This conjunction is usually left out of the translation which, in this instance, introduces the reality of the participation and applies to both elements. The celebration is initiated by the church as a body of believers, but the reality of it is experienced only by those who participate. The following verb *esthíēte* is in the second person plural present active subjunctive of *esthíō* [2068], to eat. It makes no difference how many times the church celebrates the Lord's Supper, it becomes the objective experience of those who actually eat of the bread and who drink (*pínēte*, the second person plural present active subjunctive of *pínō* [4095], to drink) the contents of the cup.

"You Clearly Declare"

The verb which we elected to translate "you clearly declare" is the verb *kataggéllete*, the second person plural present active indicative of *kataggéllō* (2605), to declare, proclaim. It is derived from *katá* (2596), an intensive preposition amounting to the meaning of "pinning down," and *aggéllō*, not found in the New Testament by itself, but meaning to declare or proclaim. The compound verb means to declare plainly, clearly, and openly. What is it that the believers clearly declare when they participate in the bread and the cup?

"The Death of the Lord"

"The death of the Lord" is translated from *tón*, the accusative singular masculine article of *ho* (3588), the; *thánaton*, the accusative singular masculine noun of *thánatos* (2288), death; *toú*, of the, the genitive singular masculine article of *ho*, the; *Kuríou*, Lord, the genitive singular masculine noun of *Kúrios* (2962), Lord. This phrase is found nowhere else in the New Testament. It refers to the voluntary death of the Lord.

How could the Lord, which means the Supreme Master, be put to death? We must never forget that the Lord died voluntarily, and in reality no one put Him to death. We refer the reader to our discussion in verse 23 of the verb *paredídoto*, which is the imperfect passive indicative with middle meaning, "He delivered Himself." In Revelation 1:18, we find a most significant statement of the risen Lord which, when correctly translated, is astonishing and revealing:

> I am He, the Living One [*ho zṓn,* the nominative singular masculine present active participle of *záō* {2198}, to live], and I became [*egenómen,* the first person singular second aorist middle deponent indicative of *gínomai* {1096}, to become] dead, and, behold, I am living unto the ages of the ages. Amen. And I have the keys of death [*thanátou,* the genitive singular masculine noun of *thánatos,* death] and of Hades.

Although Jesus was God incarnate, He allowed others to put Him to death. Their activities, however, were secondary causes of His crucifixion, for He **became** dead. He became subject to death through His own volition and power. Our participation in the Lord's Supper is a clear declaration of our remembrance of the death of the One who never ceased to be Lord (1 Cor. 8:6) and willingly died in our place for our sins. It is therefore not a commemoration of defeat, but a celebration of victory, for His resurrection followed His death and He now lives forever. The commemoration of the death of Christ is a celebration of victory because it not only reminds us of His death, but of His triumph over death! He who raised Jesus from the dead will also raise us out of death through His power (1 Cor. 6:14). In Hebrews 2:14, we read:

> "Forasmuch then as the children are partakers of flesh and blood, He also Himself in a similar manner [*paraplēsíōs* {3898} which means in like manner but not altogether the same] partook of the same; that through death [His own death which was unique, and not like ours] He might destroy [*katargḗsē,* the third person singular aorist active subjunctive of

katargéō {2673}, put out of commission] him who has [*échonta,* the one having, which is the accusative singular masculine present active participle of *échō* {2192}, to have] the power [*krátos* {2904}, dominion] of death, that is, the devil.

We all die because Satan led Adam into sin (Rom. 5:12). As a consequence of that sin, all humanity is under the curse of death; however, the death and resurrection of Jesus Christ made Satan's dominion of death ineffective for all who claim Jesus' sacrifice for redemption from their sins. This is why believers can say with the Apostle Paul, "For to me to live is Christ, and to die is gain" (Phil. 1:21). Therefore, as we examine this unique phrase, "The death of the Lord," we must recognize that it was a purposeful, willful death which resulted in resurrection, and this is the triumphant expectation of every believer. This is the death that we clearly and openly declare every time we participate in the Lord's Supper.

"During the Time Till He Comes"

I translated this statement in this way because the adverb *áchris* (891) means "till," but implies the duration of time until the period of grace is finished. There is another adverb used in the New Testament which is also translated "till." It is *méchris* or *méchri* (3360) which means "till" as it marks the terminus, not as the time in between the beginning and the terminus. Paul wanted to emphasize that this period of grace from the time that Jesus died on the cross until the time He will come back in triumph at His Second Coming (1 Thess. 4:13–18) is the appropriate time to remember the triumphant death of Christ.

After *áchris,* till, comes the word *hou,* of which, the genitive singular masculine relative pronoun of *hós* (3739), which, implying the noun *chrónou* (5550), time. The Apostle is very careful not to mention the time at which the Lord will come back again when the celebration of the Lord's Supper will cease, for then it will not be necessary for the believers to be reminded of Christ's death. That time of the Lord's coming may be a secret, but it is imminent. The conjunction that follows is *án*, the "if" of reality, equivalent to *hótan* (3752), when. The "if" conjunction which introduces a subjective possibility is *ei* (1487). Therefore *án*, which is used here, introduces the certainty of the Lord's coming. It is equivalent to *héōs* (2193), an adverb of time meaning "until" or "when." There is no doubt about the coming of the Lord as a reality. The only thing that is unknown is the time of His coming. Our Lord, in His eschatological discourse on the Mount of Olives in Mark 13:33, said to His disciples, "Take heed, watch and pray; for you perceive [*oídate*, the second person plural perfect active indicative of *oída*, the perfect used as a present of *eídō* {1492}, to know] not when the time is." The word for "time" in Greek is *kairós* (2540), opportune time or season. This is different than the chronological time which is *chrónos*. We do not know what would be the most appropriate season to expect the coming of the Lord. In the previous verse, Mark 13:32, the Lord said, "But of that day and that hour knoweth no man, no, not the angels which are in heaven, neither the Son, but the Father." This is a difficult statement, but not without explanation. The Lord was merely attesting to the fact that when he took on Himself the nature of man, He consequently put himself under certain human limitations, including not knowing the time when he would return. That He set limits on the expression and evidence of His divine nature and glory during His incarnation is seen quite clearly in the transfiguration.

The verb is *élthē*, the third person singular second aorist active subjunctive of *érchomai* (2064), to come. The word *élthē*, referring to the Second Coming of the Lord, is rare in the New Testament. It is used in Matthew 25:31, but in that verse it is used with *hótan* (3752), when: "When the Son of Man will come in His glory." It does not in any way mean **if** He comes, but **when**

He comes. However, the Lord is repeatedly referred to as "the coming One" (*erchómenos*; see also Matt. 24:30; Mark 13:26; Luke 21:27; John 1:15, 27; 3:31; 6:14; 11:27; 12:13; Rev. 1:4, 8; 4:8). Also, instead of the participle *erchómenos* or *erchómenon also* we have the present indicative used, "I am coming" (*érchomai*), or "He is coming" (*érchetai*; see Matt 24:42, 44; Mark 13:35; Luke 12:40; John 14:3, 18, 28; Rev. 16:15; 22:7, 12, 20).

"Till He comes" therefore must refer to a definitive coming of the Lord which is the rapture of the church delineated in 1 Thessalonians 4:13–18. It is then that the Lord will come to take the living saints unto Himself and to raise all the saints who have died previously. To be with the Lord will be a moment of glorification and ultimate victory at which the transformed saints (1 Cor. 15:51–55) no more need to remember the Lord's death. Rather, they will then proclaim the victory song against death, "Death is swallowed up in victory! O death, where is your sting? O grave, where is your victory?" (vv. 54, 55).

LESSONS:

1. The celebration of the Lord's Supper should never be routine.
2. Every time it is celebrated it should remind believers of what it cost the Lord Jesus to redeem them from sin.
3. The expression "the death of the Lord" ought to convey to every Christian that Jesus, being Lord, could not really be delivered unto death by anyone other than Himself (v. 23).
4. The Lord delivered Himself unto death, for being alive, He became dead (Rev. 1:18), yet now through the resurrection He is alive forever.
5. The death of the Lord was not the common death of a common individual, but the unique death of the Lord of lords (1 Cor. 8:6).
6. The death of the Lord is to be celebrated until the Lord in His glory comes for His saints to rapture them unto Himself (1 Thess. 4:13–18). Death will then be swallowed up in victory and be remembered no more.

1 Cor. 11:27 | *Unworthy Participation in the Lord's Supper*

Accordingly thus, he who would eat this bread or drink the cup of the Lord unworthily shall be guilty of the body and of the blood of the Lord.

First Corinthians 11:23–26 speaks of the celebration of the Lord's Supper as a memorial service of His death. The conclusion of that passage of Scripture is that this celebration is for believers only, and it is to remind them that their redemption is based on the offering of the body of Christ which was crucified and thus became the propitiation for man's sin. The objective reality of the sacrifice of the body of Christ must also be applied individually through faith. It does not benefit unbelievers to partake of the bread and the cup of the Lord without the objective sacrifice reflecting subjective faith. The blood that was shed on Calvary's cross is profitless if it is not individually appropriated to cleanse one's heart from sin (1 John 1:7, 9). Every time a believer participates in the Lord's Supper, he clearly declares that what the Lord came to do has been accepted in his own life. It is not the remembrance of just any body, but the body of the Lord Jesus Christ which is sacred (*hósion* [3741]) and which did not see corruption (Acts 2:27, 31). Furthermore, the body Jesus Christ took upon Himself was the same as that of humans, but yet without sin and its consequences (Heb. 2:14;

4:15). Communion, then, is partaking of that which symbolizes a unique body and it is also a declaration of experience of the power of the unique blood of that body.

"Accordingly Thus, He Who Would Eat This Bread"

"Accordingly thus" translates the adverb *hṓste* (5620), a conjunction derived from *hōs* (5613), as, strengthened by the enclitic particle *te* (5037) which serves to connect more closely the following clause with the material preceding it. Thus we are urged to carefully consider the meaning of the Lord's Supper as we study the following verses.

The next word is the singular relative pronoun *hós* (3739), who. This ascribes personal responsibility to the one who participates in the Lord's Supper. It is followed by the conjunction *án* (302) which is a contraction of *eán* (1437), the "if" of reality which necessitates that the verb "would eat" be in the subjunctive mood *esthíē* of the present tense of the verb *esthíō* (2068), to eat. Therefore, the correct translation of the phrase would be "he who would eat," which indicates any particular time that this is done. Not only does our verse point out individual responsibility, but also individual performance. This would lead us to believe that each individual believer bears his own responsibility each time he takes the bread to eat in celebration of the Lord's Supper.

The Apostle is not speaking of any bread, but of **the** bread of the Lord's Supper. It particularly speaks of *toúton* (5126), this, the accusative singular masculine demonstrative pronoun of *hoútos* (3778).

"Or Drink the Cup of the Lord Unworthily"

Observe that we have the little word "or" (*ḗ* [2228]) here, which is a disjunctive particle ascribing the same importance to the eating of the bread as to the drinking of the cup. The two elements are of equal importance in the Communion service. The hypothetical conjunction of reality *án* used in the eating of the bread is implied also with the verb "drink"; and so we have, "He who would drink," again assigning individual responsibility to this special act. The believer personally should be careful lest at any time he would participate in the cup of the Lord unworthily.

We need to examine the adverb *anaxíōs* (371) which occurs here and in verse 29 and is found only in the Textus Receptus. This adverb is derived from the adjective *anáxios* (370) which, in turn, is derived from the privative *alpha* (*a* [1]) meaning "without," and *áxios* (514), worthy. The noun *axía,* worth or value of a thing or of a person, is not found in the New Testament. The adverb *axíōs* (516) is the opposite of *anaxíōs* and means appropriately, worthily, as becomes a person or a thing. *Anaxíōs* means without worth, unworthily, or in an unbecoming manner. Such an individual who partakes irreverently, not ascribing the genuine value and meaning that the Lord's Supper should have for a believer, partakes unworthily.

For us to understand the meaning of this adverb, however, we should understand the meaning of the noun *axía* as contrasted with the synonym *timḗ* (5092), honor or attributed value. Honor attached to any item may be deemed of higher value than deserved because of what that item means to an individual. The actual value of a watch, for instance, is that which a person would have to pay to procure it in the marketplace. If the watch belonged to a beloved and deceased family member and is treasured, it has an attributed value much higher than its real value. It would not be given up for any amount of money.

The Lord's Supper has a basic value for the believing Christian, but this value increases, or should increase, as time goes on and the believer remembers the suffering of Christ on his behalf. As the Lord becomes more precious to us as believers, so should the commemoration of His sacrificial death. If, for instance, one participates in the Lord's Supper and has bitterness and unforgiveness in his heart for fellow believers or for others, then that person is participating unworthily. The death of the Lord clearly declares that our forgiveness from sin has been great indeed, in fact, beyond our comprehension. Does your participation in the Lord's Supper clearly declare that you have forgiven others as the Lord has forgiven you? (See Matt. 6:14, 15; 18:35.)

As in the previous verse, the Lord's Supper ought to remind us that it proclaims "the death of the Lord." Uniquely so, the cup of Communion is called the "cup of the Lord" (*toú Kuríou* [2962]). It is a unique cup clearly indicating a unique death. It is not the cup that belongs to one believer or church only, but it belongs to the Lord and many believers partake of it. Every believer, having experienced the power of the cleansing blood of the Lord Jesus, has the right to participate in the ceremony.

Participation in the cup of the Lord is unworthy if one claims Christ's forgiveness as being exclusively for him or his group and denies it to others who also believe. Faith in the blood of Jesus Christ is the only requirement necessary to make a person a believer and a participant in the cup of the Lord. We read in Acts 5:14, "And believers were the more added to the Lord, multitudes both of men and women." Our negative attitude toward other believers can disqualify us from participating in the cup of the Lord worthily. The Lord is the common Lord of all believers, and it is His body of which we are all members (1 Cor. 12:13).

We partake of the Lord's Supper unworthily if we do not recognize the value (*axía*) of the other members as we associate with them in the body of Christ. Paul, in 1 Corinthians 12:14–29, writes about the necessity of having different members in the body of Christ to accomplish that which God so designed for them. In verse 25 he writes, "There should be no schism in the body; but that the members should have the same care one for another." The phrase "should have the same care" uses the verb *merimnṓsi*, the third person plural present active subjunctive of *merimnáō* (3309), to show concern, be anxious. The verb *merimnáō*, as well as the noun *mérimna* [3308], is neutral in meaning, but is used in both a good and bad sense. Hence, we are instructed not to be overly concerned and to cast all our concerns on Him (Matt. 6:27, 31–34; 1 Pet. 5:7; Phil. 4:6), but we are to be sincerely concerned about the welfare of others (Phil. 2:20). The phrase "for one another" also refers to the body of Christ including all the various multitudes who belong to it because they have been cleansed by the shed blood of Christ. The word *allḗlōn* that is used is from the adjective *állos* (243) which means another of the same kind, referring, of course, to other believers. Although we fulfill different functions as designed by the Lord Himself, we must remember that we are all given the same grace (*cháris* [5485]) but different *charísmata* (5486) or gifts which emanate from that grace. Therefore, if one feels himself to be above any other member of the body of Christ because he or she functions differently and variably, he participates in the Lord's cup unworthily.

"Shall Be Guilty"

The verb "shall be" is *éstai*, the third person singular future indicative of *eimí* (1510), to be. This is a straightforward prediction of certainty and not a mere possibility. He who participates in the bread and the cup of the Lord declares by the very act that he has fellowship (*koinōnía* [2842]) with the body of Christ (1 Cor. 10:16). When we become believers, we are joined mystically to the body of Christ, and by virtue of that union we become related to each other as believers. We have a common Father and are brothers and sisters (1 Cor. 12:13; Eph. 4:4). Each member belongs not only to the Lord, but to the other members (Rom. 12:5) of the body. In Ephesians 4:3,

Paul says, "Endeavoring [*spoudázontes*, the nominative plural masculine present active participle of *spoudázō* {4704}, to diligently pursue] to keep the unity of the spirit in the bond of peace." This is the only place in the New Testament that the expression "the unity of the spirit" is used. In verse 13 we read, "Till we all come in the unity of the faith, and of the knowledge of the Son of God, unto a perfect man, unto the measure of the stature of the fullness of Christ." Therefore, we see that Paul speaks of the unity of the spirit and the unity of faith. It is just as if he were to say that anything that we may do in any way that adversely affects the unity of the spirit and the unity of the faith implicates us. The word for "unity" is *henótēs* (1775), oneness. These two references, Ephesians 4:3, 13, are the only ones where the word *henótēs* is used. It is used first in regard to the Spirit, and secondly, in regard to the faith. It is correct here to capitalize the word "Spirit," referring to the Holy Spirit as a supernatural means of achieving unity. Faith is that human faculty used by the Holy Spirit to make it possible for man to have peace with God and, in turn, unity with fellow believers. Therefore, Paul speaks here of the Holy Spirit and faith as a spiritual means of receiving the blessing of God. *Henótēs* is spiritual unity and not physical attachment. It is not the attachment of an individual to a local church that causes spiritual unity.

There is another Greek word that is not used in the New Testament but has evolved in the Greek language, even up to Modern Greek, which means union by physical attachment. That is the word *hénōsis*. There can be union by physical joining, but that is not spiritual *henótēs*, unity. In order to have unity, one must have the supernatural activity of the Holy Spirit and of faith, and thus be born again. There can be spiritual unity only among people who have been born again from above (John 3:3, 7). In explaining the difference between a physical (*hénōsis*) union and unity that is spiritual (*henótēs*), our Lord said, "That which is born of the flesh is flesh; and that which is born of the Spirit is spirit. Marvel not that I said unto you, 'You must be born again'" (John 3:6, 7).

The Greek word translating the word "guilty" is *énochos* (1777). It is an adjective from the verb *enéchō* (1758) or *enéchomai*, metaphorically meaning to be entangled, to be implicated, derived from the preposition *en* (1722), in, and the verb *échō* (2192), to have. In the King James Version in Matthew 5:21, 22 and Mark 3:29, *énochos* is translated "to be in danger of"; in Matthew 26:66; Mark 14:64; 1 Corinthians 11:27, and James 2:10 it is translated "to be guilty of," and in Hebrews 2:15 we find it as "subject to." What our verse declares is that if any individual, at any time, would eat of the bread and drink of the cup of the Lord without being conscious that these elements represent the body and the blood of the Lord Jesus who was crucified for his sins, he implicates himself as an offender.

"Of the Body"

As Christians participate in the Lord's Supper, it is of utmost importance that they understand that they belong to one body, the body of Christ. Paul very specifically, in Ephesians 1:22, 23, says, "And has put all things under His feet, and gave Him to be the Head over all things to the church, which is His body, the fullness of Him that fills all in all." In Ephesians 5:30 he says, "For we are members of His body, of His flesh, and of His bones." Anything that disturbs the functioning of the body is wrong, and those who contribute to the dysfunction of the body are guilty of wrongdoing. We must beware of such dysfunction not only in our relationship with Christ, but also in our relationships with other believers. Again Paul stresses in Romans 12:5, "So we, being many, are one body in Christ, and everyone members one of another." A safe measure to avoid being guilty of the body is not to partake of the Lord's Supper if we have any bitterness or any ill feeling toward another member of the body of Christ. In fact, every time we are about to take Communion, we ought to examine our hearts and pinpoint who are the ones in the body of Christ that we may have differences with and settle those differences. It is not enough that we merely justify our ill-feelings against our brothers in Christ, we must confess it as sin and forsake it and, inasmuch as possible, seek to make things right with our fellow believers. The oneness of the body can be preserved only if we do what the Apostle Paul says in 1 Corinthians 12:25, 26: "That there should be no schism in the body; but that the members should have the same care one for another. And whether one member suffer, all the members suffer with it; or one member be honored, all the members rejoice with it." We become guilty of the body, that is the church, if our interpersonal relationships with any other member hinders that member from performing his duty, and thus cause the whole body to function improperly.

The same unity should exist among believers as exists between God the Father and God the Son. As our Lord prayed in His high priestly prayer in John 17:23, "I in them, and Thou in Me, that they be made perfect [*teteleiōménoi*, the nominative plural masculine perfect passive participle of *teleióō* {5048}, to reach the goal] in one; and that the world may know that You have sent Me, and have loved them, as You have loved Me." Anything that a believer may do that would hinder a fellow member of the body of Christ from reaching his or her goal, and thus doing his or her part as a member of the body of Christ, makes that person guilty of causing dysfunction within the body. God has not made us all uniform, but diverse, and only as we assist each other to perform his or her function is unity preserved. A careful reading of 1 Corinthians 12 will reveal that each member has his or her separate function in the body of Christ, but functions that are complementary to the other functions rather than contrary. Although each member of the body differs from the other in its function, all must work together for the unity and comfort and growth of all. One thing that we, as members of the body of Christ, must understand is that God is the One who makes us to differ from another and that we have nothing that we have not received (1 Cor. 4:7).

"And of the Blood of the Lord"

Paul emphasizes the fact that there is unity in the body of Christ because all members have been cleansed by the same blood. It is necessary for us to understand that it takes the miraculous power of the blood of Christ to create the new nature within us, and it is just as beautiful a miracle that the new nature does not produce uniformity but unity. How boring it would be if every flower and every tree and every animal and bird and human being were exactly alike!

LESSONS:

1. Each time we participate in Holy Communion we are to examine ourselves, not only regarding our relationship with the Lord, but our relationships with other members of the body of Christ.
2. Many wrongly justify their differences with other members of the body of Christ by not considering them to be children of God.
3. We must realize that participation in the Lord's Supper represents the oneness of the body of Christ achieved through the miraculous power of His shed blood.
4. If we participate in the Lord's Supper unworthily, we shall face judgment (2 Cor. 5:10).

1 Cor. 11:28 | *Self-Examination before the Lord's Supper*

But let a man examine himself, and so let him eat of the [that] bread and drink of the [that] cup.

Partaking of the Lord's Supper is a serious matter and a believer should not partake with a lighthearted attitude. If we harbor unconfessed sin or resentment and bitterness against a fellow Christian, we are inviting judgment against ourselves.

"But Let a Man Examine Himself"

This verse begins with the verb *dokimazétō*, the third person singular present active imperative of *dokimázō* (1381), to examine. Since it is in the singular, it means that each person should examine his own life rather than the lives of others. To strengthen the idea of self-examination, there is the reflexive pronoun *heautón*, which is the accusative singular masculine third person of *heautoú* (1438), of himself. Paul wants to be sure that each one turns his eyes introspectively instead of focusing on others. Our attitude toward others affects us more than the attitude of others toward us. We must examine ourselves before we take Communion to be certain that we have nothing against a fellow member of the body of Christ. This is something that we and only we can do.

This is not the only Scripture passage where self-examination is expressly indicated for the believer. Second Corinthians 13:5 also says,

> Examine yourselves [*heautoús*, the accusative plural masculine third person reflexive pronoun of *heautoú*, of himself; *peirázete*, the second person plural present active imperative of *peirázō* {3985}, a synonym of *dokimázō*, to test, but with the difference that *peirázō* may disclose shortcomings] whether you be in the faith; prove [*dokimázete*, the second person plural present active imperative of *dokimázō*, to test with the expectation of proving worthiness] your own selves. Know you not your own selves, how that Jesus Christ is in you, except you be reprobates?

The first imperative of this verse concerning self-examination is to try yourself (*peirázete*) whether you are a believer or not. In 1 Corinthians 11:28, however, we have a difference. This verse tells us to examine ourselves so that we can participate in the Lord's Supper worthily. Do we attribute proper worth to the celebration of the Lord's Supper? Do we clearly declare to others the value of the death of Christ? *Dokimázō*, however, refers to introspection. We quote R. Martin Pope in the *Dictionary of the Apostolic Church*, edited by James Hastings under the term "Self-Examination":

> The purpose of self-examination [*dokimázō*] carries with it the suggestion that the scrutiny will end in acceptance of approval, while *peirázō* more commonly indicates a test which will issue the disclosure of what is defective and evil. But this distinction is not always obvious, nor can it always be pressed, for in 2 Corinthians 13:5 Paul uses both words together.

In our verse under examination, the verb *dokimazétō*, being in the present active imperative, means that one should test himself constantly to see whether or not he is worthy to participate in the Lord's Supper. It is not sufficient to do it only once. It is to be done constantly because there are new people being added to the body of Christ who are our brothers and sisters, and our attitudes toward others can change from time to time.

The verb is also found in the present imperative singular in Galatians 6:4, but there it speaks not of examining oneself, but examining his work: "But let every man prove his own work." This phrase is translated from *dokimazétō*, let one test; *tó* (3588), the (a neuter article); *heautoú*, his own, the genitive singular masculine third person reflexive pronoun; *érgon*, the nominative singular neuter noun of *érgon* (2041), work, that is, that which one has done. Just as a man is to examine his own life, he is also to examine whether his own work will pass the standard set by God. It seems that if we spent more time examining ourselves and our works, we would have little time left to scrutinize others.

Self-examination then is to be practiced before and after partaking of the Lord's Supper. Why? Because we shall be held accountable for our own guilt. We must each face Christ when we appear before His tribunal (2 Cor. 5:10). The more careful our self-examinations are during our earthly sojourn, the fewer unpleasant surprises we shall face on that day.

The Ransom for Our Sins

But what will happen if we, as believers, appear at Christ's tribunal with unconfessed sin?

In the New Testament, there is often a great deal of confusion when two different words are translated by the same English word. The word "ransom" is *lútron* (3083) which comes from the verb *lúō* (3089), to loose. Christ set us free from sin by paying the ransom with His own blood, which was the price set by the Father. This word occurs only twice, in Matthew 20:28 and Mark 10:45. However, the compound word *antílutron* (487) which is derived from the preposition *antí* (473), in lieu of, in return, and *lútron*, a ransom, occurs only once in the New Testament in 1 Timothy 2:6; thus it is something standing in lieu of a ransom. However, in both places it is translated by the same word, "ransom." If, however, the same thing was meant, the same word would have been utilized.

It behooves us to carefully examine 1 Timothy 2:6 and its context to find out what the *antílutron* truly is and not equate it with the *lútron*, ransom. In the fourth verse, Paul expresses the desire of God to have all men come to the saving knowledge (*epígnōsis* [1922]) of the truth. Then in verses 5 and 6 he says, "For there is one God [*Theós* {2316} without the definite article which refers to deity] and one Mediator between God and men, the Man Christ Jesus who gave Himself a ransom for all." God the eternal Son became man so that blood could flow in His veins which could be shed on the cross.

It is noteworthy that the Apostle speaks of the Incarnate Christ as "Christ Jesus." Throughout the duration of His incarnation, He did not cease to be God. The appellation "Christ" represents His deity and "Jesus" represents His humanity. The name Jesus Christ in the Gospels is found in Matthew 1:1, 18; Mark 1:1; John 1:17, etc., but He is not called Christ Jesus until we come to Acts 19:4. This is after His resurrection which was the evident proof that as the Incarnate God He was Christ first, and then Jesus. And so, after His resurrection, we find the term "Christ Jesus" in Romans 3:24; 8:2, 39; 15:5; 1 Corinthians 1:2; Galatians 3:26; 4:14; Philippians 2:5; 3:3, 8; Colossians 1:4 and Hebrews 3:1. Then we come to 1 Timothy 2:6 where the word *antílutron* is used. It is noteworthy that in both Matthew 20:28 and Mark 10:45, it deliberately says that He gave His own soul as a ransom (*lútron*) for many (*pollṓn*, the genitive plural masculine adjective of *polús* [4183], much), whereas in 1 Timothy 2:6 the noun *antílutron* is used: "Who gave Himself a ransom [*antílutron*, a representative ransom or in lieu of a ransom] for all [*pántōn*, the genitive plural masculine adjective of *pás* {3956}, every one in a specified group for whom He died effectively, therefore referring to believers]." This explains 1 Timothy 4:10 which speaks of "the Savior of all men, especially of those that believe."

The rest of 1 Timothy 2:6, "to be testified [against us] in due time," is extremely important if we understand the words that are used. We must carefully translate the words *tó martúrion* (3142). *Tó* is the neuter article "the," and most translations have rendered the neuter noun *martúrion*, a testimony **against** the defendant, as being the same as the feminine noun *marturía* (3141), a testimony **for** the defendant. Basically both words mean a testimony which is given in court. However, there is a difference, for there are usually two kinds of testimony: for and against the defendant. James Strong, in his dictionary, has treated them separately. *Marturía* is the favorable testimony in order to prove the good character of someone, whereas *martúrion* is a condemnatory testimony (see Luke 9:5; 21:13; 2 Cor. 1:12; 2 Thess. 1:10; 1 Tim. 2:6; James 5:3). In 1 Timothy 2:6 the word is *tó martúrion*, that which will serve as condemnatory witness. It is the witness which will be given in due time, at the right season (*kairoís*, the dative plural masculine noun of *kairós* [2540], season). This is the time or times of opportunity as distinguished from *chrónois*, the dative plural of *chrónos* (5550), a space of time. First Timothy 2:6 speaks of "their own seasons" (*idíois*, the dative plural masculine adjective of *ídios* [2398], his own, pertaining to oneself). This expression is found only here and in 1 Timothy 6:15 and Titus 1:3. It means in the seasons pertaining only to believers who are judged for every time they received communion, and not to unbelievers. There are seasons in our life of faith when we as Christians do or say things of which we shall be ashamed in the day of judgment, at the coming of Christ (2 Cor. 5:10). There will be an instantaneous acknowledgment of such sin, but we shall find that the ransom (*lútron*) by the blood of Christ will also serve as a representative ransom (*antílutron*) for the sins of our life of faith (Matt. 10:32, 33; Luke 12:8, 9). Such will be the sins of believers who take Communion but do not attribute the proper value to the blood of Christ as not only forgiving their own sins, but also the sins of others whom they may hold on to in bitterness. These sins will ultimately be revealed and all circumstances pertaining to them. Believers will understand that Christ's blood was also a representative ransom for the sins of others and that Jesus does not need to repeat His sacrifice to redeem them from such. The *lútron* will also serve as the *antílutron*, that is, the ransom will also serve as the representative ransom.

But Paul wants us to examine ourselves here and now while we have the opportunity to correct our attitude toward others. He is not teaching about others correcting their attitudes toward us, but about us correcting our attitudes toward others. If we fail to do this before partaking of the Lord's Supper, it is not a sin that will be held against us eternally, for the unity of the spirit will ultimately prevail in eternity among believers who could not agree here on earth. It is up to us, however, to examine our attitudes beforehand and make adjustments accordingly so that we will not be ashamed at the coming of Christ. This is why the verb *dokimazétō* is in the present imperative, let him examine himself constantly. We do not know when our lives will end, so it is better to keep our hearts always pure so that we will not be ashamed when we stand before the Judgment Seat of Christ.

Following in Christ's Footsteps

In the matter of self-examination, before we as believers participate in the Lord's Supper, we should also have in mind 1 Peter 2:21 which speaks of the suffering of Christ for our redemption and the necessity of following His example, "For even hereunto were you called: because Christ also suffered for us, leaving us an example, that you should follow His steps." The first thing that this verse declares is that we were called of God who took the initiative to do so through the Holy Spirit. This was made possible because Christ suffered for us, satisfying the Father's ransom price.

The rest of 1 Peter 2:21 also requires explanation: "leaving us [*hupolimpánōn*, the nominative singular masculine present active participle of *hupolimpánō* {5277}, to leave behind, which is found only here]; an example [*hupogrammón*, the accusative singular masculine noun of *hupogrammós* {5261}, a pattern to be traced over or copied as if left by a teacher for pupils to copy or trace], that you should follow His steps [*íchnesin*, traces, the dative plural neuter of the noun *íchnos* {2487}, the mark or imprint left by the feet]." The verb that is used in the phrase "that you should follow" is *epakolouthḗsēte*, the second person plural aorist active subjunctive of *epakolouthéō* (1872) which comes from the preposition *epí* (1909), upon (used as an intensive), and *akolouthéō* (190), to follow. This verse teaches us that Christ died for us, and through belief in His death we receive a new nature (2 Pet. 1:4), but this is not the end of the story. Jesus also lived such a perfect life that He left behind traces that we should follow.

We have all heard the illustration of the little boy following his father through the snow, and saying, "Look, Daddy, I am walking in your footprints." Are you following in Christ's footprints? Indeed, in applying this verse in relation to 1 Corinthians 11:28, we arrive at the conclusion that it is our right as children of God who are redeemed by His precious blood to partake of the body and of the blood of the Lord in His Supper. But every time we exercise that right, we ought to examine ourselves whether we are walking in His footsteps and in His teaching, especially concerning the forgiveness of others.

As we examine ourselves, we are to remember that we are still human beings, although redeemed by the grace of God, and that we may fall short in following in His footsteps. This is why our text says, "Let a **man** [*ánthrōpos* {444}, a human being] examine himself." The Apostle Paul intimates here that we should not, in spite of our redemption, forget the fact that we are all still human beings. Even as redeemed men, we ought to recognize that sin is present in us as it was in Paul as we read in his confession in Romans 7:14–25. Scripture aptly describes sin as a serpent, for a serpent usually lies hidden and undetected until it strikes. We may come to the Lord's Table believing that all has been settled between God and us through Jesus Christ, but the question that we should ask ourselves is whether the same peace that exists between Christ and us also exists between us and our fellow believers. Only then should we partake of the Lord's Supper, meditating on the fact that Christ's death brought us forgiveness and should motivate us to forgive others.

"And So Let Him Eat of the [That] Bread and Drink of the [That] Cup"

"And so" in the text is *kaí* (2532), and, even; *hoútōs* (3779), thus, so. This adverb connects what has been said previously in this verse to what follows. It connects the testing of ourselves to see whether we have followed Him in the example that He gave us before we participate in the bread and cup of the Communion service. The "of" (*ek* [1537], out of) indicates to us that we partake of one bread and one cup. But the privilege does not belong to us alone, for it is shared with other believers with whom our unity (*henótēs* [1775]) should be intact. If each believer exercises honest and sincere diligence in his examination, then, indeed, the unity of the Spirit (Eph. 4:3, 13) and the unity of the faith will be maintained.

<u>LESSONS</u>:

1. It is the personal responsibility of each individual believer to examine himself before he or she participates in the Lord's Supper.

2. It is indeed the right and duty of each believer to participate in the Lord's Supper if his or her heart is pure before God.
3. Each child of God should study Christ's example and endeavor to trace His life as exactly as possible (1 Pet. 2:21).
4. Only if the believer can come to the Table of the Lord without malice in his or her heart against anyone should he or she participate in the Lord's Supper (1 Cor. 4:12; 1 Pet. 2:23).

1 Cor. 11:29 | Discernment May Save You from a Crime

For he who eats and drinks unworthily incriminates himself by eating and drinking, not discerning the body of the Lord.

In verse 27, we were admonished not to partake of the Lord's Supper unworthily. We do this when we fail to attribute true value to the death of Christ which brought forgiveness to us and enables us to forgive those who have offended us. We are each responsible for our own selves.

In verse 28, we are admonished to examine ourselves as fallible human beings, redeemed by God's grace, to see whether we are worthy to participate in the remembrance of Christ's death. We are admonished to have intact our relationship with Christ and others within the body of Christ.

"For He Who Eats and Drinks Unworthily"

In verse 29, Paul tells us what the implications are if we should participate unworthily by having unconfessed and unrepentant sin or any bitterness in our heart toward other members of the body of Christ and of the local church. Therefore, the inclusion of the word "unworthily" (*anaxíōs* [371]) ought to be accepted as in the Textus Receptus and the Majority Text. It is missing, however, from the Critical Texts although it follows logically.

Our verse definitely speaks of the one who eats and drinks unworthily.

"Incriminates Himself by Eating and Drinking"

"Incriminates himself" is to be understood with the verbs "eating" and "drinking."

If we are to translate this phrase in the same way as the King James Version does, "eateth and drinketh damnation to himself," we imply that the damnation is actually in the eating and drinking, but in reality, it is in our attitude while eating and drinking. One reason it is called the "cup of blessing" and "the fellowship of the body of Christ" in 1 Corinthians 10:16 is that the eating of the bread and drinking of the cup brings great blessing to many.

What I translated as "incriminates" comes from the word *kríma* (2917), crime, which, in most instances, implies a proven crime and therefore the commensurate punishment due it. This word, and all the rest of the related words found in this passage of verses 29 to 32, are derived from the verb *krínō* (2919), to judge. In verse 29, we find the noun *kríma* and the verb *diakrínō* (1252), to distinguish; in verse 31, it is in the middle voice meaning to separate oneself; and in verse 32, we have the verb *katakrithō̃men*, the first person plural aorist passive subjunctive of *katakrínō* (2632), to condemn.

We shall examine each word as we come to it, but here in verse 29, we are told that if an individual partakes of the bread and of the cup unworthily, harboring bitterness and an unforgiving spirit for fellow believers, he brings upon himself a proven crime. Certainly a willful crime cannot escape punishment, whatever that punishment may be, if it is not confessed and forsaken.

The noun *kríma* here in verse 29 also entails the punishment determined by God for a crime committed by man. God is not to be held responsible as the arbitrary imposer of such punishment. The responsibility lies squarely on the individual believer who participates in Holy Communion in an unworthy manner. The "unworthy manner" is not specifically detailed nor is the punishment. Nevertheless, it is appropriate to the crime even as justice would demand. The punishment is left up to God because only He is omniscient and knows the heart of the believer and the extent of the bitterness and the damage it causes to the individual and to the body of believers.

"Not Discerning the Body"

This word "not" is *mḗ* (3361), the relative "not." In verse 28, the believer who is asked to examine himself is called "man," which is translated from *ánthrōpos* (444), human being. Although the believer still has human imperfections, his experience of the new birth qualifies him to sit at the Lord's Table. As a fallible human, he may eat of the Lord's Supper unworthily, for it is impossible for any human being to fully comprehend the meaning and the importance of partaking in the Lord's Supper.

With this in mind, it is important for us to examine the verb "discerning" (*diakrínō*, to discern, discriminate). It means to distinguish wherein something is harmful. It derives from the preposition *diá* (1223), through, and *krínō*, to conclude, judge, determine. *Diakrínō*, therefore, means to see through and to make the proper judgment. The Apostle Peter used this word in his speech at the Council of Jerusalem in Acts 15:9 in speaking of the Gentile and Jewish believers. He said, as the New International Version and the Revised Standard Version have it, "And He made no distinction between us and them, by faith having cleansed their hearts." The word "no" is translated from *oudén*, the accusative singular neuter adjective of *oudeís* (3762), none, making the accusative mean "in nothing." It comes from the absolute negative *ou* (3756); the adversative particle *dé*

(1161), but; and *hén*, the accusative neuter of *heís* (1520), one. Thus *oudén* means that "in absolutely nothing" did God distinguish or discriminate (*diékrine*, the third person singular aorist active indicative of *diakrínō*) between the Jews and the Gentiles, for it was by faith that they both had their hearts cleansed. In Acts 10:34, Peter said to the Gentile Cornelius, "Of a truth I perceive that God is no (*ouk* [again the absolute negative]) respecter of persons."

A synonym of *diakrínō* is *diaphérō* (1308), to be different from or superior to. This is why the Christian church in apostolic times branded certain things as *adiáphora*, nonessentials, showing that Christians can be different and distinct one from the other but still maintain those things that are essential to the faith. When we look at the Christian church, we find something that we hold in common and that binds us together. This, of course, is the faith of Jesus Christ which brought regeneration to us as a result of the Lord Jesus Christ giving His body and shedding His blood on the cross for the remission of our sins. This is essential to our faith.

The story is told of a Christian in an Arab country who was being pursued by a mob of fanatic Muslims intent on killing him. He turned the corner of the street and dashed into a store and on into a back room, thinking he could escape through a back door. Much to his surprise, there was no back door. He stood there trapped with nowhere to go. Quickly the owner of the shop followed him to find out what was happening. "I am a Christian," he answered, "and they want to kill me." "I am a Christian, too," said the storekeeper. "Hide under this, and I will send them away." He hid there until darkness fell and then managed to escape. A common love for the Lord immediately binds Christians together even though in practice they are not all uniform. Our uniformity consists in the fact that we are children born from above.

Paul was referring to this concept when he said that we bring judgment upon ourselves when we partake of the elements of the Communion service while we have resentment and bitterness in our hearts toward others who are different from ourselves. We are wrong, therefore, when we accept some as believers and reject others as unbelievers because they are different in nonessentials. Are not many of us in this category? We do not discern between what is essential and should be unifying, and what is nonessential and unimportant among believers. Paul, in Ephesians 1:23; 4:4, 12; 5:30, certainly affirms that all believers belong to the same body of the Lord. But just as the human body is made of many members, each one differing in appearance and function, so is the Body of Christ (1 Cor. 12:12–31).

"Of the Lord"

The Textus Receptus and the Majority Text have "of the Lord" which the Critical Texts omit. I prefer to include this phrase because the church is a distinct organism, different from any man-made organization because the Lord has created it and He will preserve it.

LESSONS:

1. In spite of the warning that Paul gives, there are individuals who participate in the Lord's Supper unworthily. Each one bears his own responsibility for partaking of the Lord's Supper unworthily.
2. It is a willful crime that bears its own judgment.
3. An individual may disregard the consequence of disobedience since in the spiritual realm it is delayed and many times not directly visible, whereas in the physical world, the consequence of disobedience is often immediate and many times visible.
4. The believer ought to distinguish the body of Christ as a unique body made up of souls who are born again.
5. There are common characteristics of the new birth and the entitlement to become children of God.

6. Jesus Christ makes us one in faith, and in the Holy Spirit, but still preserves our individuality.
7. As the children of God we all have His nature within us, but we are not uniform in our appearance or activities. We are like the members of the body, each having diverse functions and appearance.
8. Each one of us who participates in the Lord's Supper must recognize not only our oneness with other believers in Christ, but also our diversity of function in the body (1 Cor. 12:14ff.).

1 Cor. 11:30 | *Why Some Christians Die Prematurely*

For this reason there are many weak and sick among you, and a sufficient number fall asleep.

This whole portion of Scripture has to do with the possibility of believers participating in the Lord's Supper unworthily. In the 28th verse, Paul urges each one to examine himself, not only as to his relationship with the Lord, but with others in the body of Christ. Many believers who participate in the Lord's Supper believe it is of paramount importance to examine the relationship which they have with the Lord, but ignore their relationships with other believers. Paul wants to correct this. He believes, however, that negligence to correct such a situation comes from the seemingly delayed demonstration of the anger of God at the defiance of those who partake in the Lord's Supper unworthily. They sometimes hold the philosophy that the Lord is tolerant and will not do anything to them as an immediate consequence of the error of their way.

No other epistle even mentions **the gifts** of healings except 1 Corinthians, and here Paul says, "For this reason, there are many weak and sick among you." Thus the first thing that we may assume is that sickness and even death may befall a believer due to his sin.

In James 5:14, in speaking of believers, we are told: "Someone among you is sick" (a.t.). Christians are not exempt from sickness. Sickness and even death may have a personal cause, as in Acts 5:1–11 and 1 Corinthians 11:30, or no personal cause at all. But in either case, it is evidence of the corruptibility of man as a result of Adam's sin.

"For This Reason *There Are* Many Weak and Sick Among You"

"Among you" refers to those in the Corinthian church partaking of the Lord's Supper. Significant is the use of the adjective *polloí*, the nominative plural masculine adjective of *polús* (4183), much. Paul does not give us the number of those who were sick, but he does say that there were many. In the case of Ananias and Sapphira, who were struck dead when they lied about the amount of money they received from selling a piece of land, we notice in Acts 5:11, "And great fear came upon all the church, and upon as many as heard these things." Perhaps the same thing may have happened in the church of Corinth in order to discourage the unworthy participation of believers in the Lord's Supper.

The simultaneous use of the two words *astheneís*, the accusative plural masculine adjective of *asthenḗs* (772), weak, and *árrōstoi*, the nominative plural masculine adjective of *árrōstos* (732), sick is intriguing. The word *asthenḗs* derives from the privative *alpha* or *a* (1), without, the noun *sthénos* (n.f.), strength, and the verb *sthenóō* (4599), to strengthen. The word *árrōstoi* is derived from the privative *alpha* or *a*, without, and the verb *rhṓnnumi* (4517), to strengthen. Some scholars such as Liddell and Scott, the leading lexicographers of the Greek language, and Aristotle, say that *árrōstoi* may have been those suffering with chronic diseases while *astheneís* meant those who suffered from weakness of any kind, for example, physical, psychosomatic, emotional, etc. The existence of these people who were weak and sickly may have been what necessitated the exercise of the gifts of healings in the church of Corinth.

Paul does not say that **all** the weak and the sick were so because of unworthy participation in the Lord's Supper, but that **many** of them were. Paul wanted the Corinthian Christians to realize that God was not totally intolerant of their defiant spirit, but that He allowed these illnesses to remind them that corrective steps should be taken.

"And a Sufficient *Number* Fall Asleep"

A number of them even died from their weaknesses and illnesses. The word that is used for "fall asleep" or "dying" is *koimṓntai*, the third person plural present passive indicative of *koimáō* (2837), to cause to fall asleep, to die. In the New Testament it is generally used in the middle voice which is *koimáomai* or *koimṓmai*, to fall asleep, and is used only in reference to the death of believers in view of the certainty of their resurrection (John 11:11; Acts 7:60; 13:36; 1 Cor. 11:30; 15:6, 18, 20, 51; 1 Thess. 4:13–15; 2 Pet. 3:4). This demonstrates beyond the shadow of a doubt that although this punishment was of God, it had nothing to do with the eternal salvation of the believer; nor was the punishment eternal, but temporary, and it does not annul the hope of the resurrection.

The word "sufficient" or "many," as the King James Version translates it, is *hikanoí*, the masculine plural of *hikanós* (2425), sufficient. Actually, Paul says that a sufficient number of those who were weak and sick fell asleep. In other words, the number was sufficient to impress the Corinthians of their sin and to correct their unworthy participation in the Lord's Supper. Only the Lord knew the extent of this sin, therefore only He could exact a punishment that would turn the hearts of His people from their sin.

LESSONS:

1. Christians do get sick as a consequence of the original sin of Adam.
2. For some sicknesses, Christians bear direct responsibility as a result of their disobedience.
3. The results of disobedience are not always immediate, and a delay of the consequences of disobedience may lead us to misunderstand God's justice.
4. The punishment of God upon Christians is not eternal but temporal, and may involve the loss of health or even result in death.
5. In Scripture, "sleep" refers exclusively to the death of Christians rather than non-Christians. For the believer, the hope of the resurrection does not cease to exist even in the midst of temporal punishment.

1 Cor. 11:31 | *Be Thorough in the Examination of Self*

If we, therefore, were thorough in our judgment of ourselves, we would not be judged.

In verse 29, we translated the verb *diakrínō* (1252) as "discern" or "distinguish distinctly." We learned that if we partake of Communion with unconfessed sin or bitterness against our brothers and sisters in Christ, we actually incriminate ourselves in the sight of God.

"If We, Therefore, Were Thorough in Our Judgment of Ourselves"

Here in verse 31 we again encounter the verb *diakrínō,* to judge or to examine thoroughly. However, we have replaced the adverb "distinctly" with the word "thorough" for it gives a better translation in the context of what Paul is saying in this verse. He wants us to exercise a thorough examination of ourselves. When we come to the Lord's Supper, we should not only examine ourselves in relation to the Lord, but in relation to other members of the body of Christ.

The "if" here is the subjective *ei* (1487). The word "ourselves" comes from the emphatic *heautoús*, the accusative plural masculine third person reflexive pronoun of *heautoú* (1438), of his own self. A personal, thorough examination of our own selves will save us from being judged when we stand before God.

It is worthwhile to study closely the grammatical structure of *diekrínomen*, meaning that we examine thoroughly. This word is in the imperfect active indicative which means that not only should we be thorough in our self-examination at any particular time or in the critical times of our lives, but constantly, from the past stretching to the present. This would accurately translate the phrase as, "If we, therefore, were thorough in our judgment of ourselves. . . ." This is our duty. If we feel that the Lord is constantly chastising us, it may be because we have failed in our personal duty to constantly examine ourselves. Furthermore, it is in the active imperfect which means that each person should constantly have eyes of introspection upon his or her own life. We are to examine not only our actions, but our entire beings as well.

"We Would Not Be Judged"

The verb *ekrinómetha* is also in the first person plural imperfect passive indicative tense of *krínō* (2919), judge. This is judgment that is imposed by someone else, and that is God, the righteous Judge. Jesus said that He also will judge with the Father. In John 8:16, He said, "And yet if I judge, My judgment is true: for I am not alone, but I and the Father that sent Me." This judgment is not the judgment as to whether we are believers or unbelievers, because that judgment has already been rendered and our ultimate eternal destination has been determined by that judgment. In John 3:18, Jesus said, "He that believes on Him is not condemned: but he who believes not is condemned already, because he has not believed in the name of the only begotten Son of God." As to the final destiny of unbelievers, Jesus said in Matthew 25:46, "And these shall go away into everlasting punishment, but the righteous into life eternal"; and in Matthew

25:41, "Then shall He say also unto them on the left hand, depart from Me, you cursed, into everlasting fire, prepared for the devil and his angels." All unbelievers shall suffer the basic punishment of hell and shall also be judged according to the degree of their evil as we find in Revelation 20:13: "And the sea gave up the dead which were in it; and death and hell delivered up the dead which were in them: and they were judged every man according to their works."

On the other hand, believers are not going to be judged as to their faith because the Lord has already discerned the exercise of that faith. Having cast themselves on the mercy of the Lord, their destiny is not the destiny of the devil and unbelievers, but it is heaven and Christ (John 3:18; Phil. 1:21, 23; 2 Cor. 5:1–8). Believers have the promise by Christ of the resurrection unto life, but this resurrection will be a time of detailed scrutiny of their lives (1 Cor. 3:10–15; 2 Cor. 5:10). That is when, at the judgment seat of Christ, every act and thought of our lives in the flesh will be made public. It is for this reason that the Apostle Paul insists that we make a thorough judgment of ourselves now because any sin will, upon our confession and repentance, be forgiven (1 John 1:9). A thorough self-examination and a willingness to change our attitudes and behaviors accordingly will lead to commendation by our Master who will say, "Well done, you good servant: because you have been faithful in a very little, you will have authority over ten cities" (Luke 19:17; a.t.).

LESSONS:

1. Each believer ought to examine himself thoroughly at all times.
2. The believer should never lose sight of the fact that what he does not examine and correct in this life will be judged before the throne of God.
3. Judgment is necessary by a loving God who wants to guide His children to righteousness and wants the rewards and punishments for their lives of faith to be just and proper.

4. The believer's self-examination should be not only in connection with the Lord's Supper, but should be continuous in all situations that he may display the righteousness of God.

1 Cor. 11:32 | God's Judgments Are Correctional

But being judged is as if being corrected as children by the Lord, so that we may not be condemned in our togetherness with the world.

In these studies Paul emphasizes that the judgment we receive from God is not condemnatory, but correctional. This judgment has nothing to do with our eternal salvation, but with our temporal behavior. If we do not thoroughly examine and correct ourselves, the Lord is going to intervene and correct us. He is like a teacher who, when his student makes a mistake, steps in to correct him and watches so that the same mistake is not made again. It is as if Paul were saying, Do not misunderstand the Lord. He does not want to be your judge after your death, but your teacher while you are still on this earth.

"But Being Judged Is as if Being Corrected as Children by the Lord"

This verse begins with the participle *krinómenoi*, the nominative plural masculine present passive participle of *krínō* (2919), to judge. It means that while the Lord is judging us, we should view Him as a teacher dealing with children. The word for such a teacher is *paideutḗs* (3810) from *paideúō* (3811), to instruct. The word "child" is *país* (3816), a boy or a girl, and it refers to all ages from infancy up to full-grown youth (Matt. 2:16; Acts 20:12). In the sight of God we are all growing children who need not only life, but instruction as to how we should live our lives. God does not give us spiritual life and then abandon us to survive on our own. Unfortunately, the verb *paideúō* bears more of the idea of chastisement than learning (Luke 23:16, 22; 1 Cor. 11:32; 2 Cor. 6:9; Heb. 12:6, 7, 10; Rev. 3:19), for it is learning with chastisement applied when necessary because sometimes that is the only way children are willing to learn. And when chastisement is applied because of its necessity and its value, we must not regard it as a punitive measure but as an instructive medium which comes out of love. Hebrews 12:6 says, "For whom the Lord loves He chastens [*paideúei*], and scourges every son whom He receives." Then in verse 7 the Apostle goes on to say that we should receive the chastening portion of instruction as sons who need to be conformed to the knowledge and will of God. "If you endure chastening [*paideían*, the accusative singular feminine noun of *paideía* {3809}, instruction], God deals with you as with sons [*huioís*, the dative plural masculine noun of *huiós* {5207}, son]; for what son is he whom the Father chastens [*paideúei*] not?" A careful perusal of Hebrews 12:7–10 leads to the concluding verse 11 which says, "Now no chastening [*paideía*, instruction, education] for the present seems to be joyous, but grievous: nevertheless, afterward it yields the peaceable fruit of righteousness unto them which are exercised thereby." To be judged should be viewed as instructive correction which should not bring *aischúnē* (152), shame or disgrace as having done something wrong. Rather it should bring about *entropḗ* (1791), a turning inward or introspection until it accomplishes *aidṓs* (127), an inner repugnance to a dishonorable act. Therefore, in the process of education, that which is considered shameful, at first, leads to introspection and, finally, results in conformation to godliness (from *aischúne* to *entropḗ* to *aidṓs*). We read in Titus

2:11, 12 that "the grace of God . . . teaching us [*paideúousa*] that, denying ungodliness and worldly lusts, we should live soberly, righteously, and godly, in this present world." It is never the purpose of God's correction to destroy us, but to improve us, as Paul says in 2 Corinthians 6:9, "As chastened [*paideuómenoi*], and not killed." I sometimes think that if we could look into eternity and get a glimpse of that for which God is endeavoring to prepare us, we would be so much more amenable to His instructions. A little child may object vociferously to learning to read, but if he could imagine the joy and reward it would eventually bring him, he would set about the task eagerly and diligently.

As believers we are judged by God, but this judgment is not to condemn us but to instruct us. God will use whatever chastisement He deems necessary to bring about His desired results in our lives. He chastises us as a Father who loved us enough to give His life for us.

"So That We May Not Be Condemned"

Why should we view God's judgments as corrective? "So that we may not be condemned." The first word that we must examine here is the word *katakrithṓmen*, the first person plural aorist passive subjunctive of *katakrínō* (2632), to condemn. This compound verb is derived from the preposition *katá* (2596), against, and *krínō*, to judge. Although God's instruction sometimes involves chastisement, we are not going to be condemned. His chastening is temporal and does not affect our eternal salvation.

The expression "he condemned the world" is found in Hebrews 11:7: "By faith Noah, being warned of God of things not seen as yet, moved with fear, prepared an ark to the saving of his house; by the which he condemned the world, and became heir of the righteousness which is by faith." At the dawn of history, the world fell into sin. God provided an ark of salvation which Noah built by faith for the salvation of his family, and thus all his household became heirs of righteousness. Again, we find there was only one way, and that was by faith.

The Lord Jesus, in Mark 16:16, said, "But he that believed not shall be condemned." The phrase "believed not" is the correct translation of *apistḗsas*, the nominative singular masculine aorist active participle of *apistéō* (569), to not believe. The verb here is *katakrithḗsetai*, the third person singular future passive indicative of *katakrínō*, the same verb as in 1 Corinthians 11:32. The condemnation of the world is a certainty. The instruction and chastisement which the Lord provides for us should never be misunderstood as the condemnation which awaits the unbelieving world. We, as Christians, ought to be fully conscious that we are children in training. Condemnation is determined upon the world as long as the world remains unchanged and unrepentant. However, the Lord lifts His condemnation from unbelievers when they exercise genuine faith and repent from their sin. John 3:18 makes this very clear: "He that believes on Him is not condemned: but he that believes not is condemned already, because he has not believed in the name of the only begotten Son of God." In the days of Noah only those who would not take refuge in the ark perished (Heb. 11:7). God condemns only those who do not accept the way of salvation that He has provided. If you claim that you believe, examine whether your faith is true faith in the Son of God (1 John 5:20) or a faith similar to that of demons who also believe but tremble in terror (James 2:19).

Instruction is not all pleasant. It includes God's chastisement, but the end result is peace that passes understanding (Phil. 4:7).

"In Our Togetherness with the World"

Notice the preposition used in our verse. It is *sún* (4862), conjointly together. Its meaning denotes far more intimacy than the preposition *metá* (3326), with, which means next to something, not part of it. In other words, this verse declares that if we conform ourselves to the world and mix in with it and try to please it, we demonstrate the fact that we are part of it, and we shall suffer with it in its final condemnation and destruction.

Now what does the word "world" (*kósmos* [2889]) mean in this instance? It does not mean mankind in general (1 Cor. 4:13; Heb. 11:38) or material possessions (1 John 3:17). It means human society which has proven itself hostile to Christ, the gospel, and the church (James 1:27; 4:4; 2 Pet. 1:4; 2:20; 1 John 2:15–17; 3:1, 13; 4:1, 3–5, 17; 5:4, 5, 19; 2 John 7).

The verb *katakrithṓmen* refers to the final condemnation that the world is going to experience as the result of continued unbelief. That, however, ought not to be a surprise, because it is reiterated over and over in the Word of God. The only way to be certain that you will avoid that terrible condemnation is to believe on the Lord Jesus Christ here and now.

LESSONS:

1. The Lord begins a process of training after we are born into His family. As He trains us, He never ceases to be a loving Father who wants to see His children grow up to maturity.
2. We must understand that we are not willing learners and God has to punish us sometimes along the way so that we may truly learn.
3. We must be sure to differentiate between the training which may include temporal chastisement that we receive from the Lord, and the final, eternal condemnation of the world.

1 Cor. 11:33 | Be Courteous in Your Gatherings

Accordingly, my brothers, when you gather together to eat, wait for one another.

In verse 17, Paul addresses the issue of church gatherings and stresses that the members should come together for the better and not for the worse. Each member is to contribute something to the common good.

In verses 18 and 19, Paul speaks of divisions within the church, and then in verse 28, he urges that each member should examine himself when partaking of Communion. This should be a private and personal searching of the soul.

"Accordingly, My Brothers"

In this verse, Paul addresses the issue of Christian behavior in social gatherings. His advice succinctly stated is to be courteous. He has in mind what was known at that time as the Sunday supper (*kuriakón* [2960], taking place on the day of the Lord [cf. Rev. 1:10]; *deípnon* [1173], supper as the main meal of the day), or love feast. The admonition to show common courtesy may arise from the fact that these love feasts had become anything but expressions of love. Verse 21 told us that during these suppers, some were selfishly consuming their meals while others were standing by hungry, and, in fact, some were even drunk.

"When You Gather Together to Eat"

To indicate the close fellowship of their gatherings, Paul used the verb *sunérchomai* (4905), to come together, as he does in verses 17, 18, 20, 33, and 34. The fact that it is in the present participle, *sunerchómenoi* shows that it occurred quite often, and Paul implies no objection to this intimate gathering. It refers to the love feast rather than the Lord's Supper with which he dealt separately in verses 23 to 26. At first, the love feast was closely related to the Lord's Supper. This was a feast celebrating the love of God that culminated in the sacrifice of Christ on the cross, the giving of His body and the shedding of His blood for the remission of sins. The love feast was also a celebration of the love that is shared among believers as a result of our Lord's great sacrifice on the cross. The fact that these communal love feasts were abused led to their cessation, whereas the celebration of the Lord's Supper maintained its dignity and importance in the Christian church.

However, it is not wrong for Christians to gather together and have occasional fellowship meals, but they must be done in love and consideration for all. At one church we attended, a number of children came from a nearby orphanage. At the yearly Sunday school picnic, each family brought its own meal, grilling steaks or hamburgers, etc., and the enticing aroma stirred everybody's appetite. But the meals were not common meals, shared by all, for some had feasts while others did not, and the children from the orphanage had only sandwiches. It is the duty of Christians to demonstrate courteous and loving concern toward each other, considering others above themselves.

"Wait for One Another"

Self-restraint is urged in our verse by two Greek words: *allḗlous*, one another, which derives from the adjective *állos* (243), another, usually of the same kind and rank; and *ekdéchesthe*, the second person plural present middle passive deponent imperative of *ekdéchomai* (1551), wait for, thus giving us "wait for one another" (see also Acts 17:16; Heb. 10:13; 1 Pet. 3:20). In church gatherings, all believers ought to be impressed by the fact that they are brothers and sisters in Christ. The members of the body may have various functions, but they have fundamentally and basically one characteristic, which is that they are born again by the grace of God. This grace makes them equal before Him (Gal. 3:28). In Romans 12:10, Paul gives advice that we ought to take very seriously: "In honor preferring one another." What is translated "one another" is the same word *allḗlous* as in "wait for one other." In Christ we are indeed all equal, yet we perform different functions. Each function has its basic value (*axía*), but the word that is used for "honor" is *timḗ* (5092), attributed value, and it refers to the honor with which we endow our fellow Christians. The Christian church consists of unequal people made equal by Christ, and each must attribute proper honor to others. In Corinth, some coming for the Sunday supper may have immediately started eating, perhaps consuming the best parts of the meal, not thinking of those who may not have had enough food of their own. Paul admonishes them to be courteous, to wait for one another. As you would like others to wait for you, you are to wait for them.

LESSONS:

1. We need solitude for self-examination (v. 28).
2. We need church gatherings, however, to become conscious that we are one body in Christ (v. 18).
3. If we are brothers and sisters in Christ, fellowshiping together at a meal can be a blessing and encouragement.
4. Our eating together and our gathering together should always be for the better and not for the worse (v. 17).
5. In our social gatherings we should exercise courtesy and wait for each other so that all may partake equally.

1 Cor. 11:34 | *The Proper Place to Meet Needs*

But if someone is hungry, let him eat at home, so that you may not gather for something that may result in your condemnation. As far as the remaining matters are concerned, when I come I shall set them in order.

Paul, of course, is not speaking here of meals specifically meant to feed the hungry or homeless. There is nothing wrong with that, for we are admonished in Romans 12:10, to "Be kindly affectioned one to another with brotherly love."

"But if Someone Is Hungry, Let Him Eat at Home"

Here Paul is making a subjective supposition, introduced by the suppositional conjunction *ei* (1487), "if". "Someone" is the indefinite enclitic pronoun *tis* (5100), anyone, someone. Paul is trying to help us recognize that the home and not the church is the place where we should satisfy physical hunger. The church should not be seen as a place of feasting and merriment, but a place to worship and have fellowship in Christ (1 Cor. 10:16, 17).

"So That You May Not Gather for *Something That May Result in Your* Condemnation"

When we gather together in church, it should be for the purpose of the edification of the whole body (1 Cor. 14:12, 26). However, there are sometimes misunderstandings which may occur, and instead of edifying the whole body, they may result in condemnation. The word *kríma* (2917) is used in this verse, as in verse 29 which is an expressed judgment of an individual in relation to another individual or a whole group. We can only periphrastically express *kríma* as "something that may result in condemnation." Gatherings have implicit dangers in them. We may say a word, cast a look, or verbally make an observation which may become a source of condemnation to ourselves or others or the whole church. We must beware of falling into such a trap.

Although Paul does not deal with every subject concerning the Corinthian's church and social life, he does mention a few specific problems, such as undue support of one church leader over another (1:12–17). He dealt with their spiritual immaturity (2:6; 3:16); their worldly wisdom (3:18–23); criticism of others (4:1–5); their resistance to following the apostolic example of self-sacrifice (4:6–21); immorality which they refused to address (5:1–13, cf. 2:3–11); going to court one against another (6:1–11); failure to differentiate between essentials and nonessentials of the Christian faith (6:12–20); the problems of marriage and divorce (7:1–40); the believers' attitude regarding meats sacrificed to idols (8:1–13); the guiding motivation of an apostle (9:1–27). Paul used Old Testament examples to help them understand the character and will of God (10:1–22). He dealt with freedom of conscience (10:23–33); hair length and head coverings for men and women (11:1–16); love feasts in the church (11:17–22), and the celebration of the Lord's Supper (11:23–34).

"As Far as the Remaining Matters Are Concerned"

Here Paul stops to say that he had not dealt with every issue affecting the lives of the believers. There were many more things which needed his attention. This fact is implied by the three words *tá dé loipá* (*tá*, the accusative plural neuter article of *ho*

[3588], the; *dé* [1161], the adversative particle "but"; *loipá*, the accusative plural neuter adjective of *loipós* [3062], remaining one), "but the remaining matters." The Apostle Paul did not enumerate or specifically name these other matters that he had not dealt with. He may have considered them private matters which the entire church body did not need to know about. Or perhaps they were matters of less expediency. Consequently, I have rendered these three words periphrastically as "as far as the remaining matters are concerned."

"When I Come"

The Corinthians knew what these matters were and so did Paul, but he did not deem it feasible to write about them; thus he promised to deal with them in person. This is translated from *hōs* (5613), until; *án* (302), if, providing an indefinite time but a willingness on his part to discuss such matters as soon as he was able to come to Corinth.

"I Shall Set Them in Order"

It is important to examine the phrase translated from *diatáxomai*, the first person singular future middle deponent indicative of *diatássō* (1299), to arrange, set in order, derived from the preposition *diá* (1223), through or thorough, and *tássō* (5021), to arrange, to set in proper order. Paul asserts that God has established an order and that he is aware of this order and has the duty to see that it is followed. In 1 Corinthians 14:40, which concludes the discussion about speaking in tongues, Paul gives a piece of basic advice: "Let all things be done decently and in order" (*katá* [2596], according to; *táxin*, the accusative of *táxis* [5010], order, arrangement, from the verb *tássō* [5021], to arrange properly). There is a divine order of which Paul (1 Cor. 9:1) knows, and he wants to have it applied in the Corinthian church. This verb *diatáxomai* does not mean to arbitrarily impose the order Paul himself wanted, but the order God ordained and that he, as an apostle, knew. In modern Greek the verb *diatáttō* or *diatássō* has come to mean "to order or command." However, in the language of the New Testament, where it is necessary for us to acknowledge that there is a divine order which must be followed, we cannot apply the meaning of a command, but of an arrangement. The verb occurs four times in Paul's first Corinthian epistle: 7:17; 9:14; 11:34; 16:1. It seems that in 1 Corinthians 7:17 and 16:1, Paul was referring to a church order which should be applied to all the churches (1 Cor. 7:17) including the churches of Galatia (1 Cor. 16:1). We can deduce from this that the order which applies to one church applies to all churches.

In 1 Corinthians 9:14, Paul says, "Even so has the Lord ordained that they which preach the gospel should live of the gospel." It is as if Paul were saying that he, himself, an apostle of Jesus Christ, would certainly not teach something contrary to what the Lord has ordained. We conclude, therefore, that there is a divine order which must be followed by the leadership of each local church, and much care must be exercised in searching out God's divine arrangement and regulation. Our order must not be different from God's order, and what applies to one church in reality applies to all churches. God does not have different standards.

LESSONS:

1. The church is the place to satisfy our spiritual hunger, whereas the home is the place to satisfy our physical hunger.
2. There is a greater danger of doing or saying something which may be misunderstood in an assembly than at home.
3. Like the Apostle Paul, we should judge what is essential to be discussed in public and what needs to be dealt with on a personal level.
4. We must recognize the order which God has set and follow it, rather than imposing our own order.

Bibliography

Blair, J. Allen. *Living Wisely.* Neptune, New Jersey: Loizeaux Brothers, 1969.

Clow, W. M. *The Cross in Christian Experience.* London: Hodder and Stoughton, 1909.

Hastings, James. *The Great Texts of the Bible.* London: Messers T & T Clark, 1912.

Hastings, James, ed. *The Speaker's Bible: The First Epistle to the Corinthians.* Vol. 2, *The Epistle to Philemon.* 208–221. Grand Rapids, MI: Baker Book House, 1962.

James Hastings, ed., *Dictionary of the Apostolic Church.* N.p., n.d.

Lightfoot, John. *Hebrew and Talmudical Exercitations.* Oxford: The University Press, 1859.

Machen, Clarence E. *Twelve Great Questions about Christ.* London: Fleming H. Revell Co, 1923.

Maclaren, Alexander. *Christ Musts.* London: Hodder and Stoughton, 1905.

Maclaren, Alexander. *St. Paul's Epistles to the Corinthians.* London: A.C. Armstrong & Son, 1910.

Matheson, George. *Searchings in the Silence.* London: Cassell and Company, Ltd., 1895.

Maturin, William. *The Blessedness of the Dead in Christ.* New York: MacMillan and Co., 1888.

Moore, Rev. Aubrey L. "The Dignity of Womanhood," In *The Churchman's Pulpit* 23 (1912) 342–344.

Morgan, G. Campbell. *The Corinthian Letters of St. Paul.* London: Oliphants Ltd., 1947.

Morrison, G. H. *The Afterglow of God.* New York: Hodder and Stoughton, 1912.

Morrison, G. H. *The Footsteps of the Flock.* London:Hodder and Stoughton, 1904.

Morrison, G. H. *The Weaving of Glory.* New York: Hodder and Stoughton.

Owen, John. *The Works of John Owen.* Vol. 1, Carlisle, PA: The Banner of Truth, 1965.

Redpath, Alan. *The Royal Route to Heaven.* Grand Rapids, MI: Fleming H. Revell, 1993.

Sadler, Rev. M.F. "Holy Communion—Self-Examination." In *The Churchman's Pulpit.* 18 (1911) 363–367.

Stalker, J. and W. H. Hutchings. *The Sermon Bible.* London: Funk & Wagnalls Co., 1908.

Truette, George W. *Some Vital Questions.* Grand Rapids, MI: Wm. B. Eerdman's Publishing Co., 1946.

Vance, James I. *The Breaking of Bread.* London: Fleming H. Revell Co., 1922.

Wray, Rev. George, M.A. "The Qualification for the Lord's Supper." In *The Churchman's Pulpit.* 18 (1911): 367–370.

Zenos, A. C. "Tradition," In *A Dictionary of Christ and the Gospels,* Vol. 2, edited by J. Hastings, 741. N.p., n.d.

Lexicons, Encyclopedias, and References for Greek Readers, from Classical and Koine Greek to Modern Greek

Byzantiou, S. D. *Lexikon tēs Hellēnikēs Glōssēs* (*Lexicon of the Hellenic Language*). Athens: Koromēla, A., 1852.

Dēmētrakou, D. *Lexikon tēs Hellēnikēs Glōssēs* (*Lexicon of the Hellenic Language*). Athens: Dēmētrakou, 1954.

Enkuklopaidikon Glōssologikon Lexikon (*Encyclopedic Glossological Lexicon*). Athens: Morfōtikē Hetaireia.

Enkuklopaidikon Lexikon Eleutheroudaki (*Eleutheroudaki, Encyclopedic Lexicon*). Athens: Eleutheroudakis, 1927.

Kalaraki, Michael and Nikolas Galanos. *Iōannou tou Chrusostomou Ta Hapanta* (*Complete Works of John Chrysostom*), 1899.

Liddell, Henry George, and Robert Scott. *Greek–English Lexicon*, as Translated and Enriched by Xenophōn P. Moschos and Michael Kōnstantinides. Athens: John Sideris.

Megalē Helēnikē Enkuklopaideia (*Great Hellenic Encyclopedia*). Pursos (Pyrsos), Athens: Hēlios.

Neōteron Enkuklopaidikon Lexikon Hēliou (*New Encyclopedic Lexicon "Hēlios"*). Athens: Hēlios.

Papaoikonomou, George L. *Lexikon Anōmalōn Rhēmatōn* (*Lexicon of Irregular Verbs*). Athens: Kagiaphas.

Stamatakou, J. D., *Lexikon Archaias Hellēnikēs Glōssēs* (*Lexicon of the Ancient Hellenic Language*). Athens: Petrou Dēmētrakou, 1949.

Works by Spiros Zodhiates

Editor, *The Complete Word Study Dictionary: New Testament*. Chattanooga: AMG Publishers, 1992.

List of Abbreviations

acc. (accusative)

act. (active)

aor. (aorist [2 aor. for second aorist])

cf. (compare)

ch. (chapter)

comp. (composition)

dat. (dative)

etc. (and so forth)

ff. (following)

gen. (genitive)

i.e. (that is)

imperf. (imperfect)

indic. (indicative)

inf. (infinitive)

KJV (King James Version)

MT (Majority Text)

mid. (middle

n. d. (no date available)

N. p. (no publisher available)

NASB (New American Standard Bible)

NIV (New International Version)

NKJV (New King James Version)

nom. (nominative)

p. (page), pp. (pages)

part. (participle, participial)

pass. (passive)

perf. (perfect)

pl. (plural)

pres. (present)

pron. (pronoun)

Sept. (Septuagint)

sing. (singular)

TR (Textus Receptus)

UBS (United Bible Society)

usu. (usually)

v. (verse), vv. (verses)

vol. (volume)

Guide to the Transliteration and Modern Pronunciation of the Greek Alphabet

Capital Letter	Small Letter	Greek Name	Trans- literation	Phonetic Sound	Example
Α	α	alpha	*a*	a	as in father
Β	β	bēta	b	v	as in victory
Γ	γ	gamma	*g*	y	as in yell (soft gutteral)
Δ	δ	delta	*d*	th	as in there
Ε	ε	epsilon	*e*	e	as in met
Ζ	ζ	zēta	*z*	z	as in zebra
Η	η	ēta	*ē*	ee	as in see
Θ	θ	thēta	*th*	th	as in thin
Ι	ι	iōta	*i*	i	as in machine
Κ	κ	kappa	*k*	k	as in kill (soft accent)
Λ	λ	lambda	*l*	l	as in land
Μ	μ	mē	*m*	m	as in mother
Ν	ν	nē	*n*	n	as in now
Ξ	ξ	xi	*x*	x	as in wax
Ο	ο	omicron	*o*	o	as in obey
Π	π	pi	*p*	p	as in pet (soft accent)
Ρ	ϱ	ro	*r*	r	as in courage
Σ	σ,ς*	sigma	*s*	s	as in sit
Τ	τ	tau	*t*	t	as in tell (soft accent)
Υ	υ	ēpsilon	*u*	ee	as in see
Φ	φ	phi	*ph*	ph	as in graphic
Χ	χ	chi	*ch*	h	as in heel
Ψ	ψ	psi	*ps*	ps	as in ships
Ω	ω	omega	*ō*	o	as in obey

*At the end of words

SPECIAL RULES FOR THE TRANSLITERATION AND MODERN PRONUNCIATION OF THE GREEK LANGUAGE

COMBINATIONS OF CONSONANTS

Small Letter	Greek Names	Trans-literation	Phonetic Sound	Example
γγ	gamma + gamma	*gg*	g	as in go
γκ	gamma + kappa	*gk*	g	as in go
γχ	gamma + chi	*gch*	gh	as in ghost

DIPHTHONGS (DOUBLE VOWELS)

Small Letter	Greek Names	Trans-literation	Phonetic Sound	Example
αι	alpha + iōta	*ai*	ai	as in hair
αυ	alpha + ēpsilon	*au*	af, av	as in waft or lava
ει	epsilon + iōta	*ei*	ee	as in see
ευ	epsilon + ēpsilon	*eu*	ef, ev	as in effort or every
ηυ	ēta + ēpsilon	*ēu*	eef, eev	as in reef or sleeve
οι	omicron + iōta	*oi*	ee	as in see
ου	omicron + ēpsilon	*ou*	ou	as in group
υι	ēpsilon + iōta	*ui*	ee	as in see

BREATHINGS (Occur only with initial vowels)

(᾿) Smooth, not transliterated or pronounced.
When words begin with vowels, it may occur at the beginning of words with every vowel or double vowel (diphthong). ἔργον—*érgon*, work; εὐχή—*euchḗ*, vow.

(῾) Rough = h.
When words begin with vowels, it may occur at the beginning of words with every vowel or double vowel (diphthong). No distinction in pronunciation from the smooth breathing. To indicate the rough breathing we use "h" in the transliteration.

(ῥ) Rho = r.

(ὑ) Epsilon = u.
When these begin a word, they always have the rough breathing. There they are transliterated rh, hu, respectively. ῥέω—*rhéō*, flow; ὑπομονή—*hupomonḗ*, patience.

Scripture Index

Mark

Luke

John

Acts

Romans